FACING DEATH

Patients, Families and Professionals

FACING DEATH

Patients, Families and Professionals

Averil Stedeford MRC Psych.
Department of Psychotherapy,
Warneford Hospital and Sir Michael Sobell House, Oxford

William Heinemann Medical Books Ltd
London

First published 1984 by
William Heinemann Medical Books Ltd.,
23 Bedford Square, WC1B 3HH

ISBN 0-433-31550-4

Phototypeset by Wilmaset, Birkenhead, Merseyside
and printed in Great Britain by Biddles Ltd., Guildford

Contents

Ellipse   vii
Preface   ix

1. Coping with cancer: one family's story   1
2. Theory and practice: the story interpreted   7
3. Talking about diagnosis and prognosis   14
4. Telling the family   26
5. The crisis of knowledge and the expectation of death   40
6. Psychological responses to physical symptoms   52
7. Psychological problems associated with treatment   59
8. Fears of dying   67
9. The fear of death and the journey to acceptance   75
10. Learning to adjust: problems involving communication
    and dependency   85
11. Adjusting to a changing role, and the detrimental
    use of psychological defences   94
12. Anxiety   101
13. Depression   109
14. Confusion   122
15. Paranoid reactions and other problems   137
16. Bereavement: typical grief   145
17. Bereavement: complicated grief   156
18. Professionals face death too   163

Index   175

To all who have come and gone,
and to all who will come or go,
sojourning at
Sir Michael Sobell House,
Oxford

Ellipse

The doorbell rings
And flowers are delivered.
Visitors arrive; creep in to see.
Even a casual passer-by will know
If this is a coming, or a going.

In the bedroom, centre of attention,
Someone small and wrinkled lies awake,
Too young to smile or speak, or even watch.
All she can do is take
Her mother's milk; cry, excrete, and sleep.
In return she gives them joy and hope,
Delight in her new life, her innocence.

Bustling woman, seldom sitting down,
Deceives herself that all she does is give
To children, parents, others who, to live
Must feed and ask, depend on her, and take.
Sometimes so much to do she doesn't know
If she is coming or going.

In the bedroom, centre of attention,
Someone old and wrinkled lies awake,
Able to smile, but lacking strength to speak.
Nappies again, and needing help to drink;
All she can do is take.
In return her eyes give out her love.
She watches with concern as others grieve
To lose her gifts, not knowing she will leave
A store of wisdom and experience.

The ellipse of life has perfect symmetry,
Wide in the middle, ends
Both gently narrowing.
There's mystery in
This similarity
of coming and
going.

Averil Stedeford

Preface

No one should ever say to a dying patient 'I am sorry, there is nothing more that can be done to help you'. The person who says this really means that he believes nothing more can be done to bring about a cure. But the patient who is facing death needs more help, not less. The caring team now has new goals: to work with the patient and his family to keep him as free as possible from unnecessary suffering, so that he can accomplish those things that seem most important to him as his life draws to its close.

Birth and death are equally natural processes. Long before the development of sophisticated medicine, society recognised that certain people had special aptitudes for watching over these events, to ensure that they progressed smoothly, and to intervene using the skills available at the time if complications arose or undue stress occurred. Today we do much the same. In relieving the physical suffering that may accompany dying, present-day care-givers have come a long way since the time when the only drugs available were alcohol, opiates, and aspirin. Now we know that with accurate diagnosis and careful selection from a range of medications, we can achieve a level of symptom control which amazes some of our patients and our less well-informed colleagues.

The emotional and psychological needs of the dying have traditionally been met by support from the family, spiritual help for those who are religious, and tender loving care from the professionals. These are as necessary and valuable as ever; but in this area too there have been developments. Sometimes the insights of psychology can supplement intuition and love, leading to more accurate understanding of the causes of distress, and more precise treatment, providing a greater measure of relief. It is as negligent to leave a patient suffering unnecessary fear, ignorance, or mental confusion, as it is to leave him in physical pain.

Seven years of working with dying patients and their families, and with colleagues who also care for them, has convinced me that the skills of psychiatrists and psychotherapists can contribute to the understanding and better management of terminal illness. I have spoken to a wide range of professionals, including fellow psychiatrists, GPs and trainees, medical and theological students, nurses, social workers and counsellors. Their attentive listening has indicated that this is an area of deep interest for them, and the questions they have regularly asked have highlighted the areas which they find most difficult. Their responses convinced me that it would be worthwhile to write down what I have learnt in order that it might be more widely accessible.

The setting from which this work comes is a continuing care unit in the grounds of a general hospital, functioning within the National Health Service, with considerable outside support. There are 20 beds for in-patients. Others are looked after by a home-care team, and many attend an out-patient clinic and the day unit. All the patients are adults, and almost all have cancer. Some come to us very near the end of their lives, but many attend much earlier, to take advantage of the expertise in symptom control which all such units are developing. They may be discharged and re-admitted several times over the course of months or even years, and some of them will choose to die at home once their problems have become more manageable.

Although the clinical experience is based on a rather specialised unit, discussions with colleagues in other hospitals and in general practice have verified that it is widely applicable. Almost all the advice about practical management which will be found in this volume could be equally useful in other settings, provided the staff concerned have the necessary interest, knowledge, and time.

One person has written this book, but the contributors are many. Patients are excellent teachers. Much of the work here is based on a research project in which 41 couples facing the prospect of death and bereavement shared their experiences with me. Many made tape recordings, and all gave permission for their stories to be told in order that others might profit. Their accounts, and those of other patients too, have had names and other details altered to preserve confidentiality, but every episode and conversation recounted here happened to real people. To all of them I offer my grateful thanks.

Acknowledgements

Almost as great a debt is owed to Dr Robert Twycross and all my other colleagues in the unit. By watching their intuitive skills, I learned much. Conversations together in staff meetings and case discussions enabled us to solve many knotty problems. We profited from our success and from our mistakes. Their support and encouragement have enabled this book to be written.

A few other people deserve special mention. Janet Mattinson, of the Institute of Marital Studies, supervised the initial research with great sensitivity. My analyst, by his gentle understanding of me, provided a setting for rich experiences which deepened my own understanding of others. Sue Owen patiently and cheerfully typed the manuscript. I am grateful to them all.

Much of Chapter 14 was first published in the *British Journal of Hospital Medicine* in 1978. The diagrams in the chapters on bereavement were first published in *Medicine in Practice*, September 1983. The material for the final chapter was published by the National Society for Cancer Relief, to whose annual conference it was first addressed. I am most grateful to those concerned for their co-operation.

Sir Michael Sobell House   Averil Stedeford
Oxford

I

Coping with cancer: one family's story

The Bradwells were not a problem family in the usual sense of the word. William was an academic and they lived in a fine house in one of the best areas of town. His French wife, Françoise, was happily settled in England, but still missed her family who lived near Paris. The couple had a son away at university and two daughters at an excellent school. Apparently they were a happy, successful family, until Françoise discovered a lump in her breast, which proved to be cancer, and which rapidly spread. Her illness had repercussions on them all, revealing psychological problems which caused them much suffering. Their story has been chosen to begin this book because it illustrates how much can be done for such a patient and family, to help them adjust and to lessen their suffering. It will be told with little comment, and will include parts of Françoise's own account, recorded for this purpose. In the following chapter, the theory behind the work will be presented and the various interventions discussed.

The GP said it was awful to visit the Bradwells' house because all the doors were closed. When he rang the bell, William emerged to let him in and show him to the room where Françoise was in bed. Then he disappeared. They had a brief word on his way out, but the couple never spoke with the doctor together. Their daughters never appeared, although he sometimes sensed that they were in the house. He was concerned for them. They must have guessed how ill their mother was, but he knew he would not be allowed to seek them out and talk to them. Often he wondered if they were listening behind their doors.

Françoise was devastated when she found a lump in her breast. She had always been frightened of illness, and this was not the first time she had suspected she had cancer. The lump was small and the surgeon decided to remove it promptly, reassuring her that he expected it to be benign. But when she awoke from the anaesthetic, William told her that her suspicion was correct. It was a malignant lump and the mastectomy which she so much feared had been done. So they shared this truth, but after that they scarcely spoke of it again. Initially she was terrified. 'Awful, completely out of my head' was the way she described her feelings to me. She made a good recovery from the operation and had a course of radiotherapy. At first all seemed to be going well. As she put it: 'Then it seemed that for a few months my health had been recovered and my mental balance was very good.'

After those few months she began to have pain in her back and x-rays revealed that the cancer had spread to her bones. She had more radiotherapy, but just as one pain subsided, another came and she felt: 'One thing after another is going. By then I was near mental breakdown. I was absolutely like an animal which had been cornered.'

I asked her how it was at home just before she came into the unit.

> 'It's hard to describe it, it was both mental and physical anguish you know. I was screaming at home, sometimes even when I was on my own during the day. I was so frightened because nothing was being done except the irradiation. Everybody was acting towards me as if they were doing what they could but I was alone, bearing with the anguish. I screamed very often when I was on my own and sometimes when my husband was there. He couldn't understand what he could do or what was the matter and it was very difficult to explain to him because at the time we couldn't communicate very much. He went to work, and every morning he left as if everything was all right. I had an appointment to go to the hospital and I would be back at such and such a time. He returned in the evening asking me about my day as if nothing had happened, and so I was pretending, and in the end I just couldn't bear it and had these screaming attacks.'

Françoise screamed too when she first came into the unit. She had pain every time we moved her, but it was not relieved as easily as we expected with the usual drugs, and we quickly came to recognise that there was a large component of fear. She was so frightened that she held herself very tense all the time, and the look on her face told us that there was more to her problem than just physical pain. I was called to help, and she was at first very sceptical that a psychiatrist would have anything to offer someone like her. Only much later could she admit that some of the screaming was sheer terror that she might die without anyone ever realising how terrible she felt and how ill she was.

The nurses noticed that Françoise seemed very lonely and had few visitors. Her husband stayed only a short time on each occasion, although we knew that his colleagues had offered to take over some of his workload so that he could spend more time with his wife. He told her that he could not let his students down, and she respected his commitment to his work. She confided to me that she would like to see him much more, and when she saw that I understood how she felt, she plucked up courage to ask him to make longer visits. This he did, dozing in a chair in her room sometimes, or bringing work in to mark. However, communication never became really open between them. One day he sought me out in the unit kitchen to ask why it was that he could talk to me about her dying, and she apparently could do so too, yet when he tried to talk to her himself, all she seemed to want from him was reassurance. We came to the conclusion that talking to a doctor about dying is painful enough, but talking to one's own husband is much harder because that involves talking about separation from someone you love.

A member of staff in the unit had a girl at the same school as the daughters of Françoise and William. Thus we came to hear that the girls were upset at school, and that their friends were concerned for them. Neither parent thought the girls ought to be told about the seriousness of their mother's condition, particularly as they were both preparing for examinations, and academic achievement was of paramount importance in that household. The parents were unwilling to consider the idea that their highly intelligent daughters might have guessed the truth about their mother. The staff put pressure on me to persuade the father to talk to his girls, and eventually I broached the subject with him. He denied that they were upset or that they might have guessed the true situation. He was affronted that I, as a comparative stranger, might know more about what was going on in his daughters' minds than he, their father, did. Rather reluctantly I told him that we had heard in a roundabout way that his daughters were distressed at school, although they were managing to cover it up so successfully at home. He was disbelieving, so I suggested that he telephoned one of their tutors to find out for himself. I do not know whether he did this, but what I do know is that father and daughters spoke for a long time in the family kitchen the following evening, and that conversation made a big difference. Later (following talks the girls had had with me in the unit), when I asked Françoise whether the relationship between William and the girls had changed, she replied:

'Very much, an incredible amount. About communication: it was an incredible sentence the other day that he used. He said that beforehand he really hadn't realised that they were women; that he thought they were still teenagers, certainly not with the maturity they have shown since. I think this maturity has been fostered by the talks they have had in the unit. It has made a great deal of difference to their communication with their father. Beforehand everybody was trying either to avoid, or hush hush, but now the air is clear. The fear and anguish seems to have been alleviated so much through truthful relationships. Beforehand everybody was trying to cover up.'

Françoise perceived her husband as a man of high intellect whose head was in the clouds, and who could not cope with the practicalities of housekeeping. She tried to protect him from the stresses of mundane life and did not realise how capable he was of rising to the occasion when necessary. When she became ill, the father and daughters began to work together in a new way. She found this very reassuring. Speaking about the girls, she said:

'That was probably part of their anguish before. They wondered how their father would cope in the event. Should I disappear, what would become of them? I am sure that was part of their fear and they have realised that he – of course it would be horrible, I don't mean it would be easy – but certainly they now realise that he could cope.

I thought before that if I disappeared, the whole place would collapse and now I can see that they are able to respond each in their own capacity to the situation. This certainly is for me a great help in my struggle to get better. I don't mean that because I realise they can cope it is an excuse for me to let myself slide down. On the contrary, it gives me more determination to fight and to adapt myself to the new situation.'

The last remark referred to the fact that she was about to go home after several months in the unit. She was free from pain and had achieved a balance between acceptance and hope, able to envisage her family coping 'should I disappear', but determined to live well for a while at home if possible.

This she achieved (and she died there a few weeks later). Normally we would have kept in touch with her and the family through our home care sisters, but on this occasion her GP and his team were very keen to take over completely. I would have liked to have maintained contact with them, but sensed that my presence in the house would not be welcome. Although she knew I would be willing to see her, Françoise never asked me to come. I later discovered that she told her husband about an occasion when she had been angry with me and declared that she never wanted to see me again. She never told William that she changed her mind the next day, and he was left with the impression that her anger had persisted. Later he told a friend that members of the unit staff had given his wife excellent care, except for the psychiatrist who was too intrusive. Probably it was he who had insisted that the GP took over, to ensure that I was excluded.

A year later I wrote to him asking if I might use excerpts of his wife's recording to illustrate a lecture I was giving. He invited me to his home and told me that his daughters now felt they had been denied opportunities to share their mother's last illness, and that they would like to hear the tape. With some misgiving, I lent it to them, offering to come and meet them to discuss any points they wanted to raise afterwards. I never heard from the girls, but their father wrote back, saying that hearing the tape was a very strange experience for him. He said that parts of it were quite untrue, and that she never screamed at home. I had believed her account because I had heard her scream in the unit. Did he suppress the memories because they were so painful, or did she, who always liked to dramatise, exaggerate her account to make sure I understood how intense her suffering was? This we shall never know.

During my visit, William told me about Françoise's time at home, and about her death. The GP and district nurse came regularly, and she remained free from pain. She had a bed downstairs, and at first she was able to move about the house quite well, taking a share in the life of the home. Often she spoke of her hope of a cure. As she became weaker, her sister came to keep her company and help with the nursing. A week before her death she told William for the first time that she knew she was dying, and immediately added 'Is there anything I can do to make it easier for you after?' Then they spoke openly and discussed where she wanted to be buried. The next day the priest came, and following his visit, hope returned once more. She became excited about a discovery that might help her even then. But it was not to be. In her own home where she had previously been so frightened, she peacefully died.

2

Theory and practice:
the story interpreted

In working with dying patients and their families, a problem-orientated approach is very useful. First of all the patient wants to talk about his immediate concerns, and plenty of time should be allowed for this. Later a more formal history may be taken to allow fuller understanding of the background to the current situation, and to ensure that vital information is not overlooked. Often this has to be left to subsequent interviews. The purpose of the first one is to establish good rapport with the patient and particularly to engage his co-operation by making it clear that something useful can be done for him. To this end it is helpful to compile a problem list, a task in which the patient may share. For the purpose of this book, a problem has been defined as an area of concern about which:

1. some definite action needs to be taken, or
2. the patient and therapist agree they should talk further, or
3. interviews with other people need to be arranged.

Progress can later be reviewed by noting the outcome of all these things. Even in the first interview, with its attendant pressures, there must be time for friendly conversation and for being silent; for the patient to ask questions and to share feelings.

The common problems faced by the dying can be considered in four groups, and these form a framework around which much of this book is written. They are:

1. communication problems,
2. direct effects of the disease and treatment,
3. adjustment reactions to enforced changes in role,
4. pre-existing social and psychological problems.

To illustrate the value of a problem list, the one that was recorded in Françoise's notes is set out below, and will be used to organise the discussion of the case.

Problem list

1. Carcinoma of the breast with multiple bony secondaries; very demanding to nurse, very afraid of pain and of being moved.
2. Communication blocked with husband and with children and between husband and children. Reluctance to let me interview them.
3. Children reported to be upset at school and concealing it from their father.
4. Has not told her mother about her illness – uneasy about this but thinking it is probably right.
5. Marital problems – she has been supportive and is now demanding; both find it hard to adjust to this change.
6. She refuses to see friends although she seems to want someone with her most of the time; she will not look in the mirror and is angry with her body for letting her down.
7. Afraid of becoming a morphine addict, and of dependency generally.
8. Fears of how she will adapt when she goes home.

Only the first two items were noted initially; all the others were added as the work progressed.

Problems in communication are very common and often the easiest to solve. The Bradwell family had many of these. How we helped the two daughters is described in the previous chapter. The son was away from home and his needs were neglected by us all. Françoise shielded her mother from the knowledge of her illness for as long as she possibly could, but confided in her sister much earlier. The work that went on with the couple deserves further discussion here.

As previously described, we soon guessed that something was amiss between Françoise and William because his visits were so brief and she seemed so upset after he had gone. He explained to her that he could not let his students down; she agreed his work was so important that he must be allowed to get on with it without the interruptions of visiting her. Here she was colluding with his defensive attempt to avoid sharing her suffering, and this meant that she had to deny her own need. Soon she began to admit that she did want to see him much more, but that she could not ask. She had always perceived herself as giver and protector, now she had to learn that it was appropriate for her to ask and take for herself.

A weekend passed after my first interview with her. On Monday she greeted me with:

> 'I have news for you – you have given me courage to talk to William. I told him I might be dead in two weeks and that I need him. The priorities have changed. Now he comes much longer.'

When she revealed her need he was deeply moved. Before, she had tried to shield him and then blamed him for being unobservant.

When she discovered the satisfaction of asking directly for attention, and getting it, she tried to make up for what she had missed and became very demanding of William. 'I am testing him – to see how much he will do for me', she said. He seemed to understand this, coping patiently and willingly with her awkward requests. Perhaps he too was making up for lost time. Later a balance was achieved. She seemed to know better that she was loved, and did not need to prove it so often. If he had to go away for a conference, and could not visit her as usual, she accepted it and no longer made querulous demands on the nurses to compensate.

So they reached a new level of understanding; but it had some obvious gaps. For a long time William believed that she had no idea how ill she was. He believed that remarks like 'I may only have two weeks to live' were purely rhetorical and did not imply any deep acceptance of the situation. He was partly right. Once, in the course of conversation, I said to her, 'If you might live only another year or two . . .' and she flew at me in a tearful rage. I pointed out that recently she had mentioned a much shorter time. '*I* am allowed to say things like that, but you must never do so. I want to forget that now', was her retort. This was the incident that had prompted her to tell William that I was too tactless to be any use as a psychiatrist, and that she never wished to see me again. After her death he was surprised to discover that I had many more interviews with her, and that she made her recording after that episode.

Perhaps she could not tell William about her continued relationship with me because I was someone who helped her not only to maintain hope, but also to accept the inevitability of her death. Once she felt better and the threat of death receded, she did not want it to contaminate her hope. Some people can achieve that impressive balance where they accept death fairly early in their illness, and this acceptance, after a period of initial grief, does not impair their capacity to live and fight for the present. For some it even enhances it. 'Since my life is going to be short, I will get all I can out of it now', they say. Others, like Françoise, are so afraid of death that they can only maintain hope by suppressing fear and denying that they are dying. William understood this better than I did at the time, so it was to him that she turned for undiluted reassurance. Perhaps she sensed that if they once spoke openly together about their knowledge that she was going to die, this defence of denial would not be available to her. She needed that desperately for she knew from experience how overwhelming fear could be for her, especially at home.

On one occasion when I told her that William wished she could share more of her feelings with him, her response was an angry one:

> 'He didn't want to talk before; he was just scared because I howled. He is an intellectual – not used to things like that. I was dying alone and he didn't know how I felt. Now he wants to talk about everything, and he will have to wait.'

The force of her reply indicates how important it was to her not to admit to him how much she knew.

He did have to wait, for over three months. As well as her need to maintain her defence, part of her reticence with him was consistent with her wish to protect him from stress. On the day that she told him she knew she was dying (only a week before it happened) she added immediately, 'Is there anything I can do to make it easier for you after?'

What followed has already been described. If Françoise and William had not been able to accept the help offered to them, it is likely that the outcome would have been very different. He would probably have continued to cope by immersing himself in his work, and she would have died isolated from him, almost certainly in hospital.

Françoise's pain was one of the *problems directly related to her disease*. Without psychotherapy, it is likely that it would never have been brought under such satisfactory control. On her tape,

Françoise spoke as if her fear of death was something in the past when she was in severe pain alone at home, thinking that no one understood and little was being done to help her. When she was admitted, we were all aware that we were dealing with a terrified woman and that it was her fear that was making it so hard for us to relieve her pain. After several weeks of being almost pain free, she had a resurgence of 'agony' which followed the suggestion that she was sufficiently better to make a visit home. She said she was eager to go, 'but of course it would be impossible since my pain has now returned'. When I suggested that she might be afraid to go home, she became angry, although I explained that such a fear was very understandable since her last few weeks there had involved so much suffering. I accepted her anger and asked her to consider the possibility that there was a connection between the return of pain and the proposed visit. Next time I saw her she commented: 'I did not know I was that sort of person – to have pain for emotional reasons. I thought only other people were like that.'

Most of the problems related to disease and treatment are dealt with directly by the specialist teams involved: surgeons, radiotherapists, etc. However, patients often appreciate an opportunity to discuss their treatment with someone who is not in charge, who understands but does not carry responsibility. Françoise sometimes refused adequate morphine and consequently suffered unnecessarily, because she regarded depending on morphine as shameful, stigmatising her as an addict. She was glad to know that the dose would not be likely to go on and on increasing, and that if something happened so that she required less, we would not have difficulty in reducing it again. She felt that it was rather ignominious to be dependent on drugs at all, but when she was reminded that some diabetics are dependent on insulin, and that patients with, for instance, rheumatoid arthritis also live far more successfully when their pain is controlled, she accepted medication with less anxiety.

Failure to adjust to limitations often causes unnecessary suffering, and here also psychotherapy proved helpful to Françoise. It was obvious she was lonely. Every time a nurse went into her room, she was kept talking and felt almost trapped there by repeated demands for time and attention. Friends kept telephoning, asking if they could visit, and Françoise repeatedly refused.

Discussing this with her helped her to realise that she felt jealous of their good health, and did not want to be reminded of what she was missing. It was summer and she did not want to hear about the tennis because she could not play. When she overcame this and made her visitors welcome, she was much less lonely, and ceased to cling to the nurses for attention and friendship. By the time she was due to go home, she had fully accepted that she would never play tennis again, and was looking forward to going to watch, hoping that perhaps her friends might even ask her to umpire.

Pre-existing problems may only become apparent in the face of a new stress such as the threat of terminal illness. Certain patterns of marriage and family life may seem satisfactory to all concerned up to that time, but cause particular difficulty in adjustment when the delicate balance is disturbed. This was the case with Françoise and William. He was a gifted man, immersed in his work, and she thought that her main task was to protect her husband from stress and support him and the children. Intelligent and lively herself, this role was too cramped for her, so she eventually found a part-time job teaching, which she enjoyed. This still provided insufficient outlet, and her family saw her as one who over-invested in all the little details of running her home; fussing over them in ways that were irritating and restrictive. Everything had to be just so. Many things that were trivial to her family were very important to her. Even before her illness, Françoise had always been very preoccupied with her appearance and her health. She tried to eat, and give to her family, all the right foods, and took every measure she knew to keep healthy and ward off the early signs of impending middle age. No wonder she would not look in the mirror as she became pale and thin, although if she had done so she would perhaps have been surprised at a new and different beauty that was emerging, reflecting her increased tranquility. She was very afraid of illness and death. Her daughters said to me: 'Mother was always thinking she had got some serious illness – she was the last person to cope with what has happened now.'

Yet she did cope remarkably well. She and her husband had more problems than any other couple in the research series I undertook, and I spent more time on them than on any other case. Over about 10 weeks, there were 20 interviews with Françoise and various members of her family, some lasting only a few minutes, but some much longer. Weighed against the benefits, it was quite a small investment. It might even be considered very cost effective, since it was probably a major factor in enabling her to be cared for at home rather than in hospital. More importantly, the case illustrates the capacity of patients to make good use of psychotherapy, and the way in which it can complement the work of all the other members of the caring team, bringing about at least partial resolution of what at first seemed a most daunting series of problems.

3

Talking about diagnosis and prognosis

Throughout most of our adult lives, we know more about our personal situation than anyone else does, and we endeavour to control the flow of information about ourselves, deciding what can be known by others and what should remain secret. When a patient consults a doctor and the ensuing investigations show that he has a serious illness, perhaps one from which he will die, the position is different. The new information is about the patient, but it is the doctor who has the control. How they proceed is determined by their assumptions about the contract between them.

The doctor–patient contract

There are at least two views about the nature of this contract. Some see it in a technical light, as a transaction between a customer and an expert. Here the patient presents himself to the doctor rather as he presents his car at a garage when he suspects that it is developing a fault. He expects thorough investigation, good treatment, and also full information about the nature of the problem and what is to be done about it. On this basis the doctor knows what to tell, and need only ask himself how he is going to give the information, and when: whether he should give it all at once or in stages. Others see the doctor more as a parental figure. Here the expectation is that the doctor will take the best possible care of the patient, and includes an assumption that he will care for the patient's emotional well-being by handling the information he has about him in the way that will be most beneficial to him in the long run. Both are contracts about trust: on the one hand, trust that the doctor will tell the whole truth; and, on the other, that he will care for the whole person. Sometimes these two will match exactly, the whole truth being the best possible thing for that patient to hear. Often they will not match so neatly and then the

14

physician has to decide what to do. If he decides in an independent or arbitrary way how much it is good for his patient to know, he is not respecting the patient's right to knowledge about himself. The dilemma is that until the patient knows what the information is and feels its impact on him, he cannot be certain whether he would have wanted to be told or not. Therefore the decision making about the flow of information has to be carried out as a delicate negotiation between doctor and patient in which the doctor tries to ascertain how much the patient wants to know and then makes his disclosures appropriately. Occasionally patients do make it clear beforehand how they think they will want information handled should they become seriously ill. They say things like, 'Don't beat about the bush with me, Doctor. Call a spade a spade.' A few others make it equally clear that they do not want to be told much about their illness, or share in decisions about treatment: 'I'm in your hands, Doctor, I'd rather leave it all to you', they say. But usually the doctor is not lucky enough to have this information beforehand, and he must feel his way. Sometimes this can be done in a fairly direct fashion by saying something like: 'I have just got the results of your tests back. Would you like us to talk about them in detail now or shall I just tell you what I think the best treatment will be for your condition?' A question put like this allows the patient to control the information coming to him and also tells him that the physician is willing to talk about the nature of the condition when the patient is ready.

Talking about diagnosis

In the early stages of any serious disease, particularly if a cure is likely, there seems little justification for revealing the diagnosis when the patient does not ask. (From the point of view of health education, it might be right to reveal the diagnosis to all cancer patients in order that cases which do well should receive as much publicity as those which do not. This argument involves weighing the needs of the individual against those of society, and is beyond the scope of this chapter.) When malignant disease does recur after treatment which was aimed at cure, the patient may reproach the doctor for not volunteering the whole truth at the outset, but he is equally likely to be grateful for having been spared months or years of anxiety. A woman whose doctor has agreed with her that her breast lump might be cancer continues to endure considerable anxiety during the period between consultation and, for example, a biopsy result. If the biopsy is positive, she knows her worry was justified, and is relieved that it was taken seriously. If it is negative, she is usually delighted that her fears were groundless, and very seldom blames her doctor for not reassuring her enough. Similarly, patients with vague and changing neurological symptoms have spoken of their relief when their doctor has at last admitted that he too was considering the possibility of multiple sclerosis.

It is seldom appropriate, in my opinion, to tell a patient he has been cured, for example of cancer, if the physician knows it is unlikely to be true. Trust between patient and physician is an essential component in the good doctor–patient relationship. Patients need to know that the doctor understands their condition and is not unduly surprised by new developments. The patient who thinks he has been cured concludes, when he has a recurrence, that his physician did not appreciate the seriousness of his disease, and he then doubts his competence to continue care. This can be avoided by explaining all the possibilities to the patient, but although this may make the doctor seem very knowledgeable, it burdens the patient with new and often unnecessary anxieties. It is preferable to reveal just enough to satisfy the patient's needs for that moment, and deal with further questions as they come. Thus, to tell a patient, 'You have a cancer which is blocking your bowel and has spread to your liver and you have only a short time to live', may be true but it would be equally true and much kinder to say, 'You had a blockage in your bowel and I have done an operation to relieve it'. If the patient asks more, well and good. If not, the discussion should end there, but opportunities for further talk should be provided later. There is a temptation to end the consultation with a comment like, 'You will be fine now', but gratuitous reassurance can be as inappropriate as gratuitous information. Either may occasionally be given for the sake of the doctor rather than the patient, because he is finding it hard to bear within himself the pain of his knowledge of the poor prognosis. Unrealistic reassurance can be effective in the short term, but later the patient will feel he has been deceived should the optimistic forecast prove to be untrue. If symptoms return, the doctor who can say 'I did know that might happen', and go on to explain what he can now do to help, convinces the patient that his condition has been understood and further developments anticipated. Eventually he comes to recognise that his doctor cannot prevent him from dying. At times he will be angry and disappointed with him for this, but if the doctor–patient relationship can survive this phase, he will be upheld by the knowledge that his doctor knows how to minimise his suffering and will care for him right to the end.

The patient who seems not to want to know

As a general rule, it is right to let the patient control the flow of information, and to assume that if he does not make use of good opportunities to ask questions, he should not be confronted with the seriousness of his condition. But there are a number of situations where this policy would not be in the patient's best interest. Sometimes the patient does not ask about his prognosis because the possibility of serious illness and death just has not occurred to him; this is particularly true of the patient who is young and fit but who nevertheless has a condition which is going to be rapidly progressive, for instance malignant melanoma which is showing no response to treatment. If he is not told until he is very ill, he is likely to regret that he did not have enough notice to enable him to plan ahead and do some essential things while he was still reasonably well.

> Ken and Jean were a young couple with two children. For about a year Ken had symptoms of weakness of his legs, which had recently become worse. Following consultation and investigation, the neurologist wrote to say that the diagnosis was almost certainly motor neuron disease. He added that he had not told the patient and was leaving this to the general practitioner's discretion, to choose the best time. Several months elapsed without the patient consulting further, and the GP wondered whether or not he should take the initiative. Naturally he was reluctant to do so, especially as he assumed his patient was fairly well and not unduly anxious. Then he saw Jean, waiting in his partner's antenatal clinic. This made him realise that the couple urgently needed to know what Ken's future was likely to be, so he called at their home and told them the neurologist's opinion. Ken had in fact been getting worse, but had thought that it was not worth consulting again since the outcome of his first visit had been so indecisive. They were understandably angry when they were told the truth. Jean felt that she could not possibly cope with another baby if Ken was likely to become

progressively more ill, and they decided on a termination. Her grief over the loss of a baby merged into her growing distress at the prospect of losing her husband. Both were resentful toward the neurologist and the general practitioner, asserting that the delay in telling them the probable diagnosis had resulted in unnecessary suffering, particularly for Jean.

Sometimes it is necessary to impress upon the patient that his illness is serious, even life threatening, so that he can understand why the doctor is recommending treatment which may make him feel worse or have undesirable and permanent side-effects such as sterility or loss of hair.

Sheila was in her late twenties and had an emergency caesarian section about two weeks before her baby was due. At operation she was found to have cancer of the ovary which had spread widely within her abdomen. Toward the end of her pregnancy she had noticed that she was bigger than with her previous baby, and got rather more tired, but she took little notice of this. The day after operation the gynaecologist told her husband of his findings and their serious significance, but they agreed to give her a little time to recover and enjoy the baby without fear before the news was broken to her. Later I asked her how she reacted: 'I was very upset and very angry that such a thing should happen to me', she said, but she emphasised that it had been essential for her to know the diagnosis: 'I was longing to be at home with the baby, and my little girl. I wanted us as a family to be together again as quickly as possible. Several weeks in hospital seemed crazy to me, especially since I felt perfectly well. If I had not known what was involved, I would certainly have refused treatment.' After she did get home, she found it very hard to come back when further radiotherapy was indicated. She told me how her family almost forced her to agree: 'You'll be dead if you don't', they said. Sheila completed her treatment and was very well when I last heard of her two years later.

Another group of patients who benefit from being told their diagnosis is composed of those who are coping unsuccessfully with the recognition of their serious prognosis while using the defence of denial. The purpose of psychological defences is the reduction of suffering, especially anxiety. If the denying patient is living as well as the limitations of his disease will allow, the defence is serving its purpose and should probably be left alone. But if the patient is saying 'There is nothing wrong with me, doctor', and at the same time exhibiting all the signs of an anxiety state, the defence is ineffective and only causes extra problems.

> Nora, a middle-aged woman who had breast cancer, became gradually more ill but steadfastly maintained that there was nothing seriously wrong with her and that she would soon be well. Yet she always looked worried, was unable to settle to anything, and had recurrent nightmares of being trapped in a box. She awoke from these feeling she was desperately trying to push up the lid and escape. All of us felt that she would be less anxious if she could admit that she knew she was going to die, and could talk to us about her fears. Yet she blocked every attempt we made to help her to talk. One day I tried to get round it by asking her opinion about the management of illness in general: 'Do you think it is ever right to tell a patient their diagnosis if they are seriously ill?' I asked. 'Oh no,' she said, 'if you did, it would make them worried and they might have nightmares.' Even then she could not make the link which would enable her to talk about herself, but eventually she did. Another patient whom she had got to know quite well died very peacefully. Nora began to talk about this and we used the opportunity to help her to admit that she too had cancer and would one day die. As soon as this could be said, she was able to ask questions about how it would happen, whether it would be painful, and how much longer she had. Following this she became almost contented, and active in a more constructive way: knitting, and helping her husband at home during the times when she was well enough to be there. The appalling nightmare ceased and did not return during the remaining six months of her life.

Changes in awareness

Nora's story leads naturally to a discussion on the changes in awareness that take place as illness progresses. Even the matter-of-fact person who asks a lot of questions and seems to take in all the answers, seldom accepts the full implication of his diagnosis and prognosis all at once. If it were possible to contemplate simultaneously all the losses that a dying person faces, the result would surely be overwhelming. So it is not surprising that most people cope a step at a time. Even this is not an orderly progression – at times of exacerbation of disease, patients face the prospect of death anew, and make further adjustments. If there is a period when they feel better, they behave and talk as if they may recover after all.

This variability in awareness can be perplexing to professional and family alike. For some patients it signifies that they are not yet ready to face the truth. Thus a discharge letter about Mrs X may tell the GP that she has been fully informed about her diagnosis and prognosis, yet when he visits her she may say, 'Nobody in the hospital would tell me what was wrong with me.' Further questioning may reveal that she remembers part of what she was told but has not grasped its significance. Or she may deny having been told anything, and her indignation may be taken as an indication that she does want information. If the GP responds by explaining it all again, he may be surprised to hear from his practice nurse a few days later that Mrs X is complaining that no one has talked to her about her illness. Such patients do not want truth, they want reassurance. They will ask around until they get an answer which is more acceptable to them, and they will cling to that. Experience has taught me to counter the comment 'Nobody has told me . . .' with a question like, 'How do *you* think you are getting on?' If the patient replies that he thinks he is getting worse, I ask him what has happened lately to make him think so. He can be gently led on to reveal that he has seen the signs for himself and drawn his own conclusions. I do not *tell* him; rather I confirm his opinion if it is correct, or refute it and explain if it is not. Thus the realisation comes at his pace.

If the same patient responds to my question with 'I *am* getting better aren't I?', I suspect that he is not ready for the truth. In order to reassure him without lying, I try to pick out any aspect of his condition which has improved, and emphasise that. 'Well, it's certainly true that your pain is much better than it was when you first came in', might be a suitable response. If he partly wants to know, he will be sensitive to what was left unsaid, and may ask more. 'But why am I losing so much weight, doctor?' If he wants to maintain his denial, he is likely to tell his family, 'The doctor agreed my pain is improving, so I must be getting better'. When he is ready, he will ask more, and take it in.

Other patients realise the full importance of the seriousness of their condition at a practical and intellectual level at the beginning. They tell those who must be told, and make necessary financial and other arrangements. Then they may surprise everyone by talking and behaving as if they will recover, perhaps planning a holiday abroad. They are using the defence of denial in a constructive way, and they are not unduly anxious.

Talking about prognosis

Almost invariably, the patient who knows that he has a terminal illness asks how much longer he can expect to live. Because uncertainty is so painful and because practical decisions have to be made, pressure is often put upon the physican to offer a firm prognosis. Yet we know that it is very seldom possible to give an accurate forecast. Patients have more faith in the doctor's word in this area than is justified, probably because they feel more secure if they have a definite time limit within which to plan. Relatives may make a great effort if they know it will be for a short time; they may be more sparing in their commitment if they have little idea of what will be involved. Sometimes they almost insist on being given a date. I respond to this by telling them that I honestly do not know, and asking them how they would feel if I made a guess. 'Supposing I said it would probably be six months', I say, 'I can imagine you going home and getting out the calendar; counting up the weeks and marking the date when the time is up. How will everyone feel as that day approaches?' As soon as they imagine themselves in that position, they withdraw their request for a date, for most people know of someone who has outlived a prognosis by a matter of years.

Paul had been ill for about two years and was getting steadily worse. In the autumn the consultant told his wife, Pamela, that he was most unlikely to live beyond Christmas. One of Paul's workmates was a close friend to both of them and often helped by offering transport and taking Paul to the pub. As the illness progressed and Paul spent more time in hospital, Pam was lonely. Their little boy missed his father and needed the company of a man. The friend, whose marriage had recently broken down, was lonely too and visited more often. Thinking that Paul had only a few more weeks to live, these two let their relationship develop in a way that they would have postponed, had they known that Paul would still be there the following summer. As Christmas passed they felt unable to 'turn the clock back'. Paul began to guess what was happening and three people were much sadder than they would have been if a prognosis had been withheld.

Even when the doctor takes particular care to be guarded, the patient tends to select what he hears according to his needs and expectations. A statement like 'You will probably have six months to a year' will be interpreted by the pessimist as 'I have only got six months', whereas the optimist may say to his family 'The doctor said I might live for years'. Patients often need to be told quite firmly that we are unable to make a useful prediction. We should offer them continuing support as they cope with uncertainty. /

> Jenny was 36 when a diagnosis of lung cancer was made. She owned a little hairdressing business, and the income from this contributed to the mortgage she and Cyril had on a rather nice new home. When she had to sell the business, they needed to know what her prognosis was. They did not want the proceeds from the sale of the business to be swallowed up in mortgage repayments, which it would be if Jenny lived for long. There was the education of the two children to think about too. So should they sell the house and buy a smaller one? But if Jenny might only live a few months, was it fair to impose on her the added strain of moving? They decided to gamble on the probability that Jenny would die before the money ran out, and that her life insurance would then cope. Money did get tight, especially as Cyril took time off work to nurse her toward the end. The couple appreciated the support their general practitioner gave them through the anxiety that this uncertainty engendered. It did work out, but only just.

Unsatisfactory communication and its results

Among the 41 couples I interviewed for research purposes,[1] 8 patients and 10 spouses were dissatisfied with the quality of communication with their general practitioner; 13 patients and 11 spouses were dissatisfied about communication with hospital doctors. Only one patient complained of being told more than he wanted to know, and he was a person who needed to maintain denial to cope with his anxiety. All the rest spoke of difficulty in obtaining information, sometimes after quite persistent attempts. Others said their complaints were not taken seriously enough. The last is a complex issue: two of these patients had carcinoma of the pancreas, which is notoriously difficult to diagnose, and three others were hypochondriacal patients with long histories, where the presenting symptom of cancer was not recognised in the plethora of other complaints. Nevertheless, doctors ought to be able to cope with patients like these, and it seemed likely that they and others had some justification for their grievances. Their resentment was exacerbated, of course, by their belief that if the diagnosis had been made sooner, curative treatment might have been possible.

A few patients who complain that their doctor has not given them enough information, have not actually asked direct questions. 'If he thought I ought to know, he would have told me', one lady said. Others thought that the doctor was 'too busy' and one even said 'He was a nice doctor, but young, and he might have been upset to have to tell me a thing like that' (she had cancer). In some cases the doctor could have made it easier for the patient to ask; in others, the responsibility for the lack of information lay mainly with the patient.

To whom do patients turn when they have made a determined effort to get information from their doctors and have failed? McIntosh,[2] in his book *Communication and Awareness in a Cancer Ward*, describes vividly how they learn from each other. They compare notes about investigations, symptoms, and treatment, and draw their own (sometimes quite wrong) conclusions. They also use non-verbal clues: how long the doctor spends with them, whether the 'round' passes them by or greets them perfunctorily, the expression on the faces of the staff, the attitudes of their relatives. 'I knew it must be serious because everyone started being so nice to me', said one man.

Two patients in my series found out by accident and suffered as a result. One, whose bed in hospital was near the ward telephone, learned his diagnosis when he overheard the housemen saying to a colleague 'Oh, I have only one new patient in today, a man with carcinoma of the colon.' The other realised for the first time what was wrong with her when a new doctor arrived at her bedside to discuss treatment. On his name-badge she read 'Department of Radiotherapy'. These two people ruminated for several days about what they had learned before they plucked up courage to ask all the questions which their new knowledge had stirred up. Understandably, both were quite angry.

Asking other professionals

Rather than resort to guessing games and subterfuges, many patients turn to other members of staff for information when their doctor has failed to answer their questions/ Some of them do so by choice. Intimidated by the consultant's manner or the size of his retinue, they feel more comfortable asking the junior doctor who examines them, the technician who takes their blood, the nurse who is making the bed, or the social worker who may have been asked to come and talk about financial matters. Both in general practice and in hospital, this asking of others can be very satisfactory, provided the staff work together as a team with a common policy. (Just occasionally, patients ask a medical student or a cleaner because they half want to know but also recognise that such a person cannot answer their questions with authority. If what they hear is too frightening, they can discount it by saying to themselves, 'She may have got it wrong, after all she is only a student'.) Usually patients choose to ask a particular person because they feel more at ease with them than with anyone else. It is our policy that, whoever the member of staff happens to be, he or she should answer the question promptly and as fully as seems right for them, provided they are certain of their facts, and they feel reasonably sure they can handle the situation. Afterwards they should report what has transpired to medical and nursing colleagues so that others also know and can follow up the conversation if necessary. If the member of staff feels inadequately equipped to answer the question, he or she should without delay find someone who can. 'I am afraid I can't tell you; you will have to ask the doctor' has sinister implications for the patient. He may have thought for several days before he dared to ask anyone at all, and he should not be kept anxiously waiting for too long./

In the course of the ordinary day's work, there arise opportunities for junior staff to learn more about talking with patients. If they can sometimes 'sit in' with seniors when this is being done, or if they can discuss their own interactions with patients with their peers and seniors, perhaps in a group setting, their own skills quickly improve, and mutual trust within the team grows. Many patients value the opportunity to talk about their illness in some detail with staff other than doctors, and provided communication within the team is good, the quality of care improves considerably. So, incidentally, does the sense of job satisfaction felt by the staff.

Problems arise when communication is poor and when policy is unclear or is authoritative but divisive. Junior staff experience

considerable stress when a patient asks direct questio
consultant has decided that the truth must be conc
him. If the nurse or houseman tells without permiss
later found out, a reprimand or worse may occur. B
settings it takes courage for a junior nurse or houseman to
challenge authority and say 'Mrs X has asked me her diagnosis
today and I think she would be better off if she were told.'
Nevertheless, this is a more constructive way of dealing with the
situation. Discussion with the consultant or ward sister may
reveal that there was other information about the patient's
background or personality which was not available to junior staff
and which was influencing the decision. Alternatively, the
consultant who is acting through prejudice or fear may be
prepared to think again, and gradually a change of policy may
follow.

In the situations described, the patient suffers too. Having
asked a question and got no answer, he judges from the evasive
response, the quick reassurance, or the embarrassed expression,
that he should not have done so, probably because the answer
would be too painful for him to bear. So he remains ignorant, but
more afraid than before.

My own research suggests that poor communication about
illness causes more suffering than any other problem except
unrelieved pain. When things go wrong, it is often claimed that
lack of time and poor working conditions are contributory
causes. This may be so, but insensitivity, a reluctance on the part
of staff themselves to face the issues involved, and ignorance are
causes too. With training and encouragement, we could do
better than this.

References

1. Stedeford A. (1981). Couples facing death; II Unsatisfactory
   communication. *British Medical Journal*; **283**: 1098–1101.
2. McIntosh J. (1977). *Communication and Awareness in a Cancer Ward*.
   London: Croom Helm.

4

Telling the family

When a patient visits the doctor with a complaint that could be the first symptom of serious illness, both of them make decisions about what to ask and what to tell. Concurrently they decide either actively or by default whether anyone else shall be informed. Bringing a relative or friend and asking that they be included in the consultation should ensure that information is shared from the beginning, but often it does not. Several of the research couples who attended together and asked direct questions reported that they had to press very hard to obtain answers. With more reticent couples, or when the patient attended alone, the doctors were commonly guarded in what they said initially, and found an opportunity to say more to the spouse later. Of the 41 research couples, 9 were told the diagnosis separately. In this small series the measure of satisfaction about communication reported by couples was not influenced by whether or not they were told together.

Telling relatives more than the patient

The practice of telling relatives more than the patient about diagnosis and prognosis is only justified if they ask and the patient, given ample opportunity, does not. When relatives are interviewed separately, they sometimes request or even insist that the patient is not told his diagnosis. This puts the doctor in a difficult position, particularly if he suspects that his patient already wants to know or is likely to ask direct questions in the future. His first duty is to his patient, but it is important to maintain good rapport with the family if at all possible.

There are a number of reasons why relatives ask the doctor not to tell, and exploring these patiently may resolve the problem. They may have been advised previously that it is unwise to reveal the truth to patients.

> Daphne, a married woman in her late thirties, had breast cancer. She was told her diagnosis at her explicit request and shared it with her husband. When her mother found out that she knew, she angrily demanded to see a doctor, saying that her daughter would be demoralised by what we had done and that we should have consulted her first. It transpired that two years previously her own husband had died of laryngeal cancer. The surgeon had strongly advised her not to tell her husband his diagnosis and she had kept the secret from him for almost two years, at great cost. She and her daughter were very close, and Daphne did not know whether to side with her mother or with us. The mother was angry with us, not only because she felt we had done something harmful to her daughter, but also because our policy caused her to question the value of what she had done for her husband.

This incident could have been avoided only if we had seen Daphne's mother as well as her husband, soon after admission. Such extended care is not always possible, but the case provides a salutary reminder that the parents of adult patients sometimes need our consideration at much as husbands or wives, and children.

Relatives may believe that the patient will lose hope and stop fighting if he knows the diagnosis. Enquiring about how he has coped with any previous crises may reveal background information useful in influencing how his questions are answered if and when he does ask. A history of previous depressive illness is not a contraindication to telling the truth; I have known some such patients cope very well. One said to me 'This is much easier than depression. Everyone knows what I have got, and they help me. When I was depressed, nobody understood.' Some patients do go through a crisis of hopelessness soon after they are told, but most emerge from this in a short time and some come out with a determination to fight which is made all the stronger by their knowledge of the odds.

Often relatives do not want the patient to be told because they know intuitively that while he remains in ignorance they can defend against their own grief by keeping up a cheerful façade. They justify this to themselves by saying that they are doing it for the sake of the patient. Like the couple in Chapter 1, they are afraid that sharing the knowledge might be unbearably painful. Quite often the patient has guessed and he too is pretending, for the sake of the family, and therefore denying himself the opportunity of asking all the questions his secret knowledge has raised in his mind.

Relatives sometimes insist that a patient does not know the truth when there are many indications to staff that he does. I have found it useful to point out to them that he seems to me to be the sort of person who has probably thought a lot about the course of his illness, put two and two together, and drawn his own conclusions. When they consider this idea they often remember little clues he has given them which they ignored before. He may have tested the family by making remarks like 'Don't assume I'll be here forever!' in a way that could either be taken seriously or dismissed as a joke. Recalling something of this kind makes relatives begin to recognise that he might already know. Often they then agree that the doctor may tactfully explore how much the patient has guessed, and answer truthfully any questions that follow. They need to be reassured that he will only go as far as the patient wants, and not take a blunt or confronting approach. They also appreciate it if he promises to inform them of the outcome of the interview. If they are left in ignorance, they are apprehensive each time they visit, wondering whether they should maintain their façade or prepare themselves for a very different sort of conversation.

Sometimes doctors advise against telling when relatives would rather be open. This causes problems of a different kind.

Marion was 39 and had a brain tumour. Her symptoms progressed rapidly and she was taken unconscious to theatre for emergency surgery within 48 hours of the beginning of her illness. The neurosurgeon could only partially excise the tumour and he told David, her husband, about her poor prognosis. Without any discussion the neurosurgeon stated that he had decided that she should be told only that she had a cyst, and that radiotherapy would cure it. Marion and David had shared everything important up to then, and David really wanted her to know as much about her condition as he did. He felt that they had faced things together in the past and would be able to do so again. But he had been so shocked by the disastrous events that had overtaken them so unexpectedly that he did not think clearly when the surgeon spoke to him, and he felt unable to object. She was very glad to hear that she would soon be much better, and although David still wanted to tell her the truth, he was reluctant to spoil her pleasure in the first good weeks.

Initially she did do well, but soon she stopped improving and began to wonder why her efforts in physiotherapy no longer produced results. When she began to deteriorate, she thought she was not trying hard enough and became depressed, and sometimes suicidal. By then her personality had changed somewhat and David felt she no longer had the resources to cope with the truth. When she came in to our care she was frightened, sometimes paranoid, and often confused. We could not tell her then because we could not be certain that she was able to concentrate long enough to take in all we said. She might have understood the bad news but been unable to accept the reassurance we could offer about the care and help that was available. We already knew that when she was paranoid we could not comfort her. So we had to agree with David that it was now too late to tell. We managed her distress as well as we could with drugs, but she died frightened and isolated. Because they had been unable to share, David could not support her as he would have liked, and he was full of regret.

When we discussed it afterwards, we recognised that knowing the truth from the beginning might have produced quite a different sequence of events. Initially, Marion would have been as sad as David, but they could have planned their limited future together. She might have been more pleased with the degree of recovery she achieved. She would not have blamed herself when progress ceased, nor made such vigorous and futile efforts to rehabilitate herself. Because she did not realise that she had a disease that could account for her deterioration, she had to find another cause, and she blamed us. Later, knowing intuitively that she was dying, she said in her paranoia 'You are killing me'.

David (and we) found all this hard to bear. Looking back, he said: 'If only the neurosurgeon had asked me how I thought Marion would take the news. I knew my wife better than he did. Of course there is a chance that I could have been wrong – but I only wish that I had at least been given the opportunity to discuss it.' So did we.

Communication between husbands and wives

Of the 41 research couples, 34 (83%) of the patients and 28 (68%) of the spouses were satisfied with the quality of communication between them about the illness. In only 26 (63%) instances were both content. Dissatisfaction in this area was not closely related to the general quality of the marriage. Some with poor marriages were nevertheless able to say all that they thought necessary to each other. A few who had 'always been close' just could not put their feelings into words, although they wanted to. This agrees with Hinton's[1] findings that patients with average or poor marriages more often tell their spouse of their awareness of impending death.

In the nine couples who were not told simultaneously, the length of time that the secret was kept varied from one week to eight months. Two never shared it at all. Marion and David's story has just been recounted. In the other case, we found it easy to comply with the husband's request that his wife should not be told. She was a very placid woman who asked no questions. Day by day she got steadily weaker, but she seemed comfortable and enjoyed visits from her large family. She died peacefully and we all agreed that to confront her with her diagnosis would have been inappropriate and indeed meddlesome.

> Gwen was different again. She discovered a lump in her breast, guessed what it was, and decided to conceal it from her husband and everyone else for as long as possible, telling me later that she did so because she hated the thought of upsetting him. She was not seen by a doctor until pain made her give in and take to her bed. By then the condition was widespread and she lived only another two weeks. When she was admitted we felt we had to tell her husband her dignosis, and he was deeply shocked. He did not reproach her then because he appreciated that she had spared him months of anxiety, but after her death it took him a very long time to get over his anger and grief that she had not let him share her suffering or care for her. 'If only I had known, I could have made it so much easier for her', he said repeatedly.

Whenever patients or their spouses were unhappy with the quality of communication between them about the illness, I offered to help. Occasionally just taking the history was enough. They each discovered they could talk about their problems more easily than they expected. Sometimes they then spoke together about the questions I had asked them, and so communication became established. Where the breakdown was part of a long-standing marital problem, it was not always possible to bring about such change, but if it was a direct response to the crisis of the illness or to the clumsy way information had been handled by staff, interventions were often effective. Some couples accepted my suggestion that I see them together. When I did, I usually found that as soon as I had started them talking I could slip away, leaving them to share their grief and new closeness in privacy. Other husbands or wives wanted to initiate the vital conversation themselves, and invariably they were pleased with the outcome. Some wept together for the first time and discovered it was safe to do so. The dying partner was the main comforter in some instances. He or she had been quietly facing the problem alone for weeks or months, and had achieved a deeper level of acceptance than the spouse had anticipated. We should never underestimate the capacity of the dying to give.

As soon as the knowledge is shared, the couple can begin to make plans. They can settle details about finances and they can ask more freely for help from the extended family. Even delicate questions like 'Do you want burial or cremation?', or 'How would you feel if I ever married again?', may be asked and answered. A husband or wife who is about to leave his or her partner with many responsibilities, particularly when there are young children, usually feels guilty. Planning how the surviving spouse will cope relieves some of this guilt, and the bereavement is also made a little easier.

> Andrew lived for just 11 weeks after the diagnosis of lung cancer was made. Mary, his wife, was a graduate, but was not working as they had a big family. Together they decided that she should return to college for a year to become a fully trained teacher. In this way her career would give her most free time when her children were at home. They worked out a way for her to finance that year, and they prepared the children for what was going to happen. Some months after Andrew's death, Mary told me 'It was knowing that I was doing what we had both planned that kept me going. It *was* awful, but I almost felt he was behind me, encouraging me. How I would have coped if we hadn't talked like that I just can't imagine.'

When a couple have just faced together the fact that one of them is likely to die, they often choose not to tell anyone else for a little while, until they have regained their equilibrium and adjusted to the situation themselves. But before long they turn their attention to the extended family. 'How shall we prepare the children?' they ask; and 'When shall we break the news to the parents?'

Telling the children

There are many variables that influence the way children are prepared, or not prepared, for the death of a parent. It would be common sense to assume that the most powerful deciding factor was the age of the child, but evidence from the 19 couples in my study who had children aged under 18 suggests that the most important factors are the parents' own attitude to death and to openness with children in general, and the amount of support they received from the extended family. One father began to prepare a little boy of 4 for his mother's death a year before it occurred. Another couple did not tell their daughter and son, aged 16 and 20, until a week before their father died.

Families who are open from the beginning seem on the whole to manage better. The case of Jenny and Cyril (see the end of Chapter 3) illustrates this. Jenny said that as soon as they had been told that she had cancer:

> 'We decided immediately that we would tell the children. They are 13 and 16. My daughter was about to go on holiday and we thought that it was best to tell her because we did not know quite how long I had to live. She was very worried. It was only fair to give her the choice. In actual fact she didn't want to go.'

I asked her how they took the news:

> 'Well obviously, my husband had to tell them. They were extremely upset of course. They had one day off school each with Cyril, then after that it has been marvellous. They seem to accept it and we talk about it quite openly. I think it is by far the best way because you talk it out of your system, and you don't mope about it too much.'

I asked whether the children told their friends:

> 'My daughter has told a few people, only very close friends. She has got a boyfriend who knows because he visits us, and his

parents have been absolutely marvellous. And she has told a few other friends, and of course a few schoolteachers.'

The O'Haras were a very different sort of family, but they too worked together incredibly well. They had four children, girls of 14 and 13 and boys of 9 and 3, when Rosa first became ill. She had breast cancer and was ill for over four years. She and her husband Pat did not share the task of telling the children for reasons to be explained later. Pat spoke to the two girls immediately and answered their questions fully; soon he told the older boy too, and later the little one. In a recorded interview he spoke of how it affected them.

> 'My kids did benefit from it, all of them did. Even the younger one, because as I thought he was able to take it, I used gradually to tell him. When she was bad or was going into the hospital I would say "Mummy is bad and Mummy may get worse, you see. You have got to get used to the idea that Mummy will get worse and she won't be able to get out of bed, she won't be able to get into the car", and he was gradually getting used to it. It was good for the kids in that respect. They learnt to live with it and it probably made them more helpful.'

Pat was interested to hear that Rosa had told me that when the youngest was only 3 he once said 'Are you going to die, Mummy?', for she had never reported that conversation to him. Occasionally during her illness, Rosa spoke as if she was fully aware of her diagnosis. But for most of the time she could not face the prospect of leaving her husband and family, and coped by using the defence of denial. When she could no longer do housework or cooking, she still liked to feel she was in charge and was not letting the family down. Pat understood this very well and explained it to the children. All five worked together to keep up the pretence they knew their mother wanted, and to maintain her morale. Pat described it this way:

> 'She was a little highly strung. I didn't think it was a good idea to tell her all the details and the children, they went along with it. I was probably very fortunate in the kind of children that I have got; they were 13 and 14 when it happened first, even at that age it was possible for me, and even with the boy who was only 9, I could sit down and explain to them. They could understand and I explained

what we would have to do in the time that was to come. They understood and they went along with it. We would only tell Mum what we thought was best for Mum to know and after that we would just discuss it among ourselves and we kept it that way. I suppose it was just owing to the kind of kids they were that they could understand like this. Their mother and I, we always from an early age brought them in on things, on everything that was happening. They probably matured very soon; they were part of everything that was going on from an early age so I think that helped them when it came to the time when their mum got ill.'

About housework he said:

'Because of the kind of medication she was on for a time, she wasn't being very realistic about things. She might think we weren't dusting too well or we weren't cleaning too well, maybe when it had just been done. But we always went along with everything she said and we always gave it to her that anything that was done in the house, whatever it was, had been done by her. If she walked into the kitchen just when some washing up had been done and she felt that she wanted it done again, well that was it. We did it and we made her feel that she wasn't cut away from the rest of us.'

Several times in the month before her death Rosa woke in the night thinking it was about to happen, and persuaded Pat to get all the children up so that she could see them. Yet when death came nearer she told him she would not want them all around her bed. She died peacefully at home during a morning while all the children were out, supported by Pat and the home-care sister who had become almost part of the family in those last weeks. At follow-up this family was doing exceptionally well.

By the time I met the Lattimer family I had seen a number who were open with their children, and I was impressed that this seemed by far the best policy. When I heard that Martin and Betty, whose children were 16 and 20, did not intend to tell them how ill their father was although he had only a few weeks to live, I had great misgivings. I assumed that as teenagers they had guessed anyway, but the Lattimers were an unusual family. The parents were warm but very authoritarian, and had brought the children up to do as they were told and ask no questions. Both children seemed young for their ages, quiet and compliant, and it was the parents' wish that none of the staff should talk to them, so I never saw them alone. Both Martin and Betty were sure that they did not realise the seriousness of the position, and were determined to spare them this knowledge for as long as possible, despite persuasion on my part to do otherwise.

The weekend before his death, Martin made a brief visit home, and told his children then. He reported to me that they did indeed express surprise as well as grief, and thanked him for sparing them so much anxiety. They said they had realised that their father was ill, but that all along they were expecting that he would recover.

This family was very grateful for the care that Martin received (though Betty told me later of her resentment at my attempt to change her mind about telling the children), and they have kept in touch with us for several years. Both children are now at work, and everything seems to be going as well as it could be. I still wonder how much they really knew. This family taught me to respect different ways of coping, and not to try to push anyone into a preconceived mould of my own.

Even by the time that a parent needed admission to our unit, 7 of the 19 couples with children had not begun to prepare them for what was to come. Many of these, like the Bradwells of Chapter 1, assumed that the children were not aware, or if they were, they were not worried. We know that Mr and Mrs Bradwell were wrong, and that the whole family benefitted from the opening up of communication.

The Harris family was not coping well either. Derek Harris had widespread cancer. He would not talk about his illness with his wife, Carol, so she could not begin to discuss with him how to talk to their children, Anne who was 10, and Gerry who was 9. There were other problems too: she was angry with the doctors over what she felt was inefficient treatment, given too late, and she was angry with Derek's parents who were estranged from him and would not come to visit their dying son. She felt she had enough to contend with already. Having two upset children on her hands would be just too much. So she concealed her anxiety from them until the day when it became evident that Derek had a secondary tumour in his brain, and she could no longer contain her distress. That night she told them that their daddy was probably going to die very soon. The two children reacted in different ways. Anne cried a lot, even in her sleep, but Gerry showed no feelings at all. This worried Carol more than Anne's tears did, and she consulted her GP, who told her to keep an eye on him. However, he seemed to her to be quite all right. Following that night, they asked of her, after visits 'How is Daddy today?' If she said 'Daddy is not very well', they said nothing. If she said 'Daddy's fine today', they said 'Oh good', and went off to play. Neither child wanted to come and visit their father (though Anne would come if her granny came too), so we had little chance to meet them. A few days before Derek died, Gerry went to bed with a tummy ache and declared that he would not get up until the doctor made him and his daddy better. He did not stick to his word, but he expressed his feelings again very clearly the night that his daddy did die. Going to a drawer he got out a pair of his father's pyjamas, put them on, and wore them to bed.

How that family coped we never knew, for Carol would not allow any follow-up. By the time they came to us there was such a backlog of problems that their defences seemed impenetrable and there was very little that any of us could do except listen and support. This seemed to help Carol in that she became much less anxious after she unburdened herself to me for over an hour. She refused to see me again, however, perhaps because she was afraid I might somehow confront her once more with all the pain she left with me.

At this stage in my experience I would hesitate to give advice about how children should be prepared for the death of a parent. It is evidently beneficial to provide the couple with opportunities to talk it over with an outsider, and to consider in that conversation what would suit their own children best. They seem glad to hear about how other families have managed, and they are reassured that children are capable of adapting. In families with younger children, supporting the parents and giving them confidence in their own ability to handle the situation well seem to be preferable to offering to talk to the children oneself. Family sessions can be very valuable for those who are prepared to accept them.

Adolescents do appreciate talking to the doctor alone, and they often reveal a much deeper understanding of their parents than most would give them credit for. Some whom I met had already asked themselves how much they should try to take the place of the dying parent, supporting the surviving mother or father or caring for younger siblings. They have to weigh this against their increasing need for independence and continuing education. Sometimes their sudden 'maturity' is a defence against grief which they would regard as childish. Promiscuity and delinquency are more extreme responses to the threat of losing a parent, or to bereavement.

If the well parent is too preoccupied in attending to the needs of the dying spouse, the children may feel doubly abandoned. The help of relatives, especially grandparents, is very valuable here, and the knowledge that they are useful assuages their own grief a little. Where there are no family members to support the children, a social worker or health visitor may help to fulfil this role for a time, until the parent is again able to give enough. Church-going families are often helped by clergy, youth club leaders etc., and some schoolteachers also make a major contribution to a child's welfare during a crisis of this kind. The routine of school can provide an area of stability while home feels insecure. Most parents make a point of informing teachers of the illness, so that due allowance is made if the child's work falls below its usual standard, or he develops other problems. All children suffer when they lose a parent, but if they are well supported and do not have to cope with too many other changes or losses at the same time (such as moving house or changing school), their natural resilience may allow them to emerge from their grief and continue their development satisfactorily.

Older couples with adult children sometimes need help too. Some of these parents also are reluctant to confide in their offspring, protecting them as if they had never grown up. Others find it hard to accept the role reversal implicit in receiving care from their children. They regard themselves as a burden, and sometimes deprive their sons and daughters of opportunities to help when they would most willingly have done so. Talking these attitudes over with the parent may help him or her to accept support from the children. If they do not, they may cause them more suffering, not less, and during bereavement they too will say 'If only I had known . . .'.

Telling parents

How soon parents are told about the serious illness of a son or daughter depends not only on the closeness of the relationship, but also on whether they are perceived as supportive or dependent. In close families there arises conflict between the wish to confide in parents and the wish to protect them from suffering, especially if they are elderly or ill. Where the parent has already had, for instance, a heart attack, and is therefore perceived as particularly vulnerable, patients say things like 'I just couldn't tell him, it might kill him.' Sharing painful information makes it seem more real and inescapable, and the apparently genuine wish to protect parents may represent a rationalisation of reluctance to face the truth or to see the parents upset. However, parents who are kept in ignorance until their child is dying or dead suffer far more shock, and are also deprived of opportunities to offer help or comfort, and to say goodbye. Most patients, when asked to consider this point of view, decide to tell.

> Jenny and Cyril, who prepared their children so well, were anxious about Cyril's mother, whose husband had died two years previously, after which she had moved to be near them. She had arthritis and depended on them for transport and for most of her social contacts. When Jenny became ill, Cyril wanted to devote most of his attention to her, and at first felt guilty about doing less for his mother. However, she was very understanding and actually discovered that she could do more for herself than she thought. A neighbour who was asked to help became a friend and introduced her to other women of the same age, so she became more part of the community. The elderly are very grieved at losing a child, sensing that the natural order of events has been reversed, and often they feel guilty at remaining alive. Cyril's mother's new friends of her own generation supported her through this experience, and enabled her to be more help emotionally to him and his children.

Where relationships are strained, the situation is different. A daughter who perceives her mother as over-protective or possessive may delay telling her for as long as possible, fearing that she will insist on coming to 'help' and will take over the household, handle the children in a different way, or alienate the husband and divide the couple. In poor marriages, and also in very young couples where the bond with the parents is stronger than the new relationship, patients sometimes turn to parents for support, leaving the spouse feeling rejected and jealous. Among my patients, a husband who was afraid this might happen dissuaded his wife from confiding by telling her that it would be cruel to distress her parents with such news.

In divided families, doctors, social workers, and others can inadvertently get caught up in rivalries and subterfuge. When relatives ask for an interview, it is wise to check with the patient first. He may wish to retain control of the spread of news through his family, and to prevent relatives who are not on speaking terms from suddenly finding themselves one on each side of his bed!

Nevertheless, secrets in a family usually cause more problems than they solve, and many people experience a great feeling of relief when they no longer have to be kept. I have been impressed by the way so many families pull together in times of crisis; brothers or sisters taking a larger share in the care of parents or children, and thus freeing the dying patient and those closest to him from unnecessary anxieties. But before the relatives can begin to do this, they must know that they are needed, so open communication is a vital step toward mobilising family resources. Under acute stress, people do not always think clearly, and tend to muddle on in isolation. The simple questions 'Who else could help you?', and 'Have you asked them?', may be necessary to start the process off.

References

1. Hinton J. (1980). Whom do dying patients tell? *British Medical Journal*; **281**: 1328–30.

5

The crisis of knowledge and the expectation of death

Almost everyone assumes that they will live to be old. Young people assume they will reach adulthood and probably marry, young adults that they will progress in their work, bear and bring up children. Later they hope to see their children marry; that they will enjoy retirement and their grandchildren. Most people, consciously or unconsciously, are looking forward to the next stage in their lives and they seldom contemplate death. A few think about it much more, or even look forward to it. They include the very old who feel they have completed their lives and perhaps outlived many of their contemporaries; depressed and disappointed people who see life as a burden and wish to escape; and those who have lost a beloved partner and expect that death will bring a reunion. But the majority of people, when confronted with illness which is likely to result in death, respond with shock, often followed by anger. They see themselves as about to be 'cut off before their time' and feel cheated of what they regard as their due. They go through what Mansell Pattison[1] calls 'the crisis of knowledge of death'. This is a time of peak anxiety when they recognise the threat of death but are uncertain about whether it is inescapable. If they accept that it is, they wonder when and how it will occur. Uncertainty seems the hardest experience of all for the psyche to bear. Once a person knows what is likely to happen, he can begin to adapt or plan accordingly. Until he knows what kind of action is appropriate, he can do nothing. Either he is helplessly paralysed or he is distressed by purposeless agitation. Some will die in this crisis: victims of serious accidents, heart attacks or strokes. Those who initially improve pass in a matter of hours or days into what Pattison calls the 'living–dying interval'. This phase follows the crisis of knowledge of death, and precedes the terminal phase. It may last for months or years, and the patient finds himself on one of four 'dying trajectories', to use the phrase of Glaser and Straus,[2,3] depending on the kind of illness he has.

Dying trajectories

The four trajectories are:

1. certain death at a known time,
2. certain death at an unknown time,
3. uncertain death but a known time when the question will be resolved,
4. uncertain death and an unknown time when the question will be resolved.

A discussion of the varying effects of each of these trajectories now follows.

Certain death at a known time

A person who sustains a very severe injury or has, for instance, a massive heart attack may know intuitively that he is very soon to die. Before he loses consciousness he may say 'I am dying, aren't I?', or give whoever is with him a message for someone he loves. In this poignant moment there is no pain and little evidence of emotional distress. Patients who have almost died, e.g. during cardiac arrest, have reported a sense of detachment. Time seems to stand still, or their life history flashes before them. They do not report fear. Others have told of 'out of body experiences' in which they have observed, without concern, the efforts of the resuscitation team working on their unconscious body. Some say they went on a journey, following a light or a benevolent figure; that they were aware of being called back, and of a reluctance to return. Accounts of this are given by Moody in his book, *Life after Life*.[4] Patients who survive such an experience often lose some of their fear of death and live more fully subsequently, as if they have learnt an important lesson from what has happened. As one put it to me, 'I feel that being alive now is a bonus – and I appreciate it more fully than I ever did before.'

When there is a longer interval between the knowledge of impending death and the actual demise, the patient shows in a very acute form the usual range of responses to crisis. Anxiety increases, solutions to the problem are sought, and anxiety mounts further as it is recognised that this is a new and insoluble problem. Panic may ensue and the patient may die struggling and afraid, or a variety of psychological defences may be brought into play to cope with the anxiety. If there is time and sufficient emotional support, the dying person gradually becomes able to abandon these, express his anger and grief at what is happening, and move toward resignation or acceptance. All this can happen in a surprisingly short time.

Mrs M. had widespread cancer and had been ill for over a year. She never asked what was wrong and was never told. Her husband had found out about her serious prognosis several months before her death. Each treatment she had made her feel better temporarily, and she always hoped that on this occasion she would remain well. However, she got worse, became bedridden, and her admission was arranged. During the first night in hospital she lay awake, thinking. Putting two and two together, she recognised the meaning of the events of the year – that no treatment produced lasting improvement and that she had changed from a fit woman to an invalid. Suddenly she became aware for the first time that she was dying. Panic stricken, she called for help. The nurse who came found her very agitated, screaming that she was going to die and did not want to; then asking for a needle to end it quickly. She repeated her request for euthanasia to end her terror, and could not be left alone for an instant. She clung to whoever was with her, yet seemed to derive no comfort from their presence.

The unit had only been open for a short time and no one on duty that night had dealt with a crisis quite like this before. The nurses' anxiety probably added to the patient's fear. To their credit, they sensed intuitively that to sedate her heavily would be an inadequate response to her need, and they stayed with her constantly until I came. It was a new situation for me too, but I managed to calm her sufficiently to get her to tell me what had happened. Her discovery that I already knew she was soon to die, and that I was concerned but clearly not overwhelmed, probably calmed her more. She asked if her husband knew too. I said I thought he did. She could not believe this, and asked me to send for him immediately. While we waited for him to come she began to tell me that they were looking forward to his retirement, that they planned to use some savings to travel abroad, and that a daughter was to be married next year. Suddenly she realised that she would miss all this, and anger at the the seeming injustice of it all flared up. She raised her voice again – 'It is not fair!' I indicated my understanding of this feeling and she quietened again. When her husband arrived in the unit, I asked her if she would be all right if I left her alone while I went to meet him, and she agreed to let me go.

I spoke briefly with Mr M. and he confirmed that he had known the diagnosis for some time, but had done his utmost to conceal it from his wife. In a crisis earlier in her life she had made a suicide attempt, and he was afraid she would do the same again. I went with him to her bedside. 'Do you know?' she asked. 'Yes, I do' he replied as he took her in his arms. They wept silently and I left them alone. When I saw him next he was wheeling in the mobile telephone. 'We are going to ring up all the family', he said. 'She wants everyone to know.' Doing this helped them to come to terms with the knowledge together.

Later in the morning he left her to attend to some business, and she slept. When she awoke she was very sad, but by evening many members of her family had arrived to say their goodbyes, all with flowers and messages. Propped up in bed, she became animated, buoyed up by being the centre of so much attention and love. Through most of the next few days she slept. When awake, she had periods of grieving over all that was to be lost, and these alternated with happy reminiscences of the good things she had enjoyed. When the nurses were alone with her she was sometimes sad, but more often cheerful, even cracking jokes. After two or three days she asked that no one should visit her anymore, except her husband. He sat with her throughout the fifth night, and in the early hours she spoke to him for the last time. She told him that she was not afraid, and that she was content except for her sadness that she had to leave him. A few hours later she died. He left the unit bowed with his own grief, but grateful and amazed that she had actually enjoyed parts of her dying, and had worked her way through to peace.

The doctor who was first called to her was very aware of her acute distress and also that she was creating a major disturbance, upsetting patients and staff alike as she shouted loudly for a needle. But he noted that she could be calmed a little by his presence, and he decided that I should be called, in the hope that somehow I could reach her in spite of her panic. The alternative would have been to 'knock her out' with a large dose of chlorpromazine or diazepam. We have since learned that a small dose of sedative may make such patients worse, impairing their self-control even more, and making them drowsy so that they cannot concentrate enough to take in what is being said to comfort or reassure them. If a sedative has to be given, a large initial dose must be used. Even in patients who are quite ill physically, 100–150 mg of chlorpromazine may be needed. As they emerge from this after a few hours, some patients are calmer, as if their psyche has made some adjustment while they were sedated. But others again present the state just described. They are less accessible to conversation than before because of the drug effect, and yet exceedingly distressed. Here the only humane option is to repeat the chlorpromazine for several doses before allowing them to emerge from the sedation again. If the patient is already near to death, this policy carries the risk that the effects of the drug may merge with the ongoing process of dying so that the patient slips into coma and dies without regaining consciousness, although after a time no further chlorpromazine is given. The patient who is not quite so ill initially may emerge from even a day or two of sedation, able to respond rather like Mrs M. In her case it is probable that giving an initial high dose of sedative would have committed us to continuing it, as she would have been most unlikely to cope rationally once her already very tenuous control had been impaired by drugs. Then all of us would have been deprived of something good. She would not have enjoyed the attention of her family; they would have missed the opportunity to say goodbye to her; and we would have been denied that opportunity to witness the resilience of human nature adapting successfully to the knowledge of death.

Almost certain death at an unknown time

The 'almost' is added to Glaser and Straus' second category because it is hardly ever appropriate to say that a patient will certainly die from a given condition. Just occasionally, the best clinicians are wrong: the diagnosis is mistaken, the widespread cancer disappears, the disease that has been so inexorably progressive remits, and it seems as if there has been a miracle. Because of this, a space must always be left for hope. To do so is not incompatible with being realistic. Those who cope well with the uncertainty of a very long illness prepare for the worst and hope for the best simultaneously. What they mean by 'the best' changes as the illness progresses. It may begin with hope that there will after all be a cure. Then the patient sets limits – the 'bargaining' of Kubler-Ross.[5] He hopes to live to see a particular event such as the wedding of a daughter. The implied bargain is that if he is granted this favour, he will accept his fate without protest. Having achieved that goal, he may choose another – 'Don't forget I have two more daughters' is the way one man put it when the oldest one was married. When the long-term future is uncertain, working toward something that is likely to be achieved quite soon leaves the patient with a sense of satisfaction, improving his morale. As the illness progresses, the goals change and the intervals shorten, until the patient comes to live a day at a time. As it becomes more apparent that he will soon die, he hopes for a peaceful death or looks forward to joining deceased relatives. Whether he believes in immortality or not, he longs for reassurance that he will not be forgotten.

> Albert, a keen billiards player, was delighted that a competition cup was to be named after him. He spoke of how he imagined his friends competing for it and talking about him after his death. The activities of his children became an increasingly important topic of conversation for him, as if he was assuring himself that he would live on through them. One day he told me that he had been too ill to attend his first grandson's christening and therefore was not in the photographs. Sensing what this meant to him, I suggested that next time the family visited, someone should take a picture of him holding the baby. Later he showed it to me. I admired it and pointed to the little child, saying that in a few years time he too might look at the picture and say 'That's my grandad'. The old man's face glowed with pleasure at such a thought.

Much of the rest of this book will be devoted to discussing in detail the recognition and management of the many problems that arise in a patient who will not recover but is not yet dying. His task is to live as well as possible, within the limits imposed on him by his disease. Those who want to help him, do so by making sure every treatable symptom is treated, and by encouraging him and his family to adapt to the changing roles and circumstances.

Only the problems peculiar to the uncertainty will be discussed here. They have already been touched on in the section on prognosis (Chapter 3), and above, where the technique of setting limited goals is mentioned as a way of achieving a sense of satisfaction through short-term projects.

Helen, a teacher with three teenage children, illustrates this. She had breast cancer with secondaries in her hip, making walking difficult. Although we thought she was too ill, she was determined to return to teaching for the autumn term. More radiotherapy gave her some relief and regular oral morphine kept her comfortable enough to cope. She wrote a play for her class to perform at Christmas time. By half-term she had developed a secondary brain tumour and kept losing her balance. Then even she realised she could not manage her lively class, and made her own decision to resign. At the end of the summer term her head teacher had doubted her fitness to return to teaching, and she took great pride in having proved him wrong.

Her next goal was Christmas. The tumour was progressing rapidly and she began to get mentally confused, which added to her distress. More radiotherapy caused the tumour to regress temporarily. She was well enough even before the course was complete to go back and watch the children perform the play she had written. She spent Christmas at home with her family, doing little but always the centre of the party. She came back to the unit weary but triumphant and decided to try to repeat the performance over the New Year weekend. She managed this too, and over these two holidays visited all the members of her large family. Early in January she returned to us satisfied. 'I have done all I intended to do', she said, 'now I will just wait and see what happens next.' She had several more brief outings but soon became drowsy and more ill. She died peacefully, knowing that her family was sharing her pride in all that she had accomplished.

The illness that goes on for years presents special problems, particularly when there have been several episodes where death seemed likely but recovery occurred. Like a cat with nine lives, the patient has cheated death repeatedly. After a number of false alarms, he and his family learn to defend themselves from the stress of recurring crises by coming to believe that he will always recover. When he really does reach the terminal phase, everyone responds with shock and acute distress, as if they were totally unprepared. Since their morale is already undermined by years of uncertainty, restricted activity, limited holidays, and perhaps chronic deprivation of sleep, they are in the worst possible position to cope, and special consideration must be given to their needs.

Uncertain death but a known time when the question will be resolved

Infants and children with congenital anomalies that may be corrected by operation come into this category. The parents of such a child know that without intervention he is likely to die of the condition sooner or later; that at the time of operation the risk of death is increased; but that if he survives that crisis, the chances of improvement or even cure are considerable. Patients with chronic renal failure who are offered a transplant, and those with progressive heart disease offered a valve replacement, are in a similar position. Through their long illness they may come to accept the probability that without surgery they will die in the foreseeable future. They suffer from preoperative anxiety, of course, but it is tempered with hope, and with relief that something decisive is being done. This is particularly true for those who find invalidism hard to bear, who would rather be reasonably well or dead.

The patient who initially survives a serious accident or warning bleed from a fragile brain artery, and then requires surgery carrying a high risk, is in a different position. Yesterday he was well and today he is critically ill. Provided he is sufficiently *compos mentis* to be fully aware of his situation, he and his family approach the operation with unmitigated anxiety, complicated by the shock and anger that typically accompany the early stages of response to the threat of death. Sometimes it is only in the postoperative phase, or even much later, that the patient realises for the first time how near to death he has been, and he then goes through a crisis of anxiety and distress as if it has just happened. If those around him are enjoying their relief that the danger is over and that he is recovering, they may find his distress incomprehensible or even irritating. They need to understand that he may be doing an important piece of psychological work, for which he needs time and support.

It is one of the developmental tasks of the maturing psyche to come to terms with death. Particularly in the first half of life, awareness that we are mortal remains unconscious most of the time, hidden from us by our normal psychological defences, but influencing us in ways of which we are oblivious. In the face of such a clear threat as a serious accident or a subarachnoid haemorrhage, these defences may be breached. The patient imagines what would have happened if he had died, and grieves over the possibility of leaving his work incomplete, his spouse alone, or his children orphaned. His relatives similarly may imagine themselves bereaved, and they also grieve. Since even contemplating the *possibility* of these things happening causes so much suffering, it is not surprising that the patient and relatives become anxious to do all they can to prevent such an occurrence in reality. They become vigilant for signs of any new threat. Patients show undue concern about new symptoms and relatives become very protective. Both may experience unusual separation anxiety and want to be together as much as possible. These responses are only pathological if they become entrenched, and therapy should be directed at preventing this.

There are three possible outcomes. With the passage of time the defences may be rebuilt, and anxiety diminishes as the awareness of the possibility of death is again suppressed into unconsciousness, where it continues its subtle influence. Such a patient recovers to his former state, scarred only by an increased vulnerability to anxiety in situations that remind him of the danger he was once in.

A few patients actually grow through this experience, attaining a new poise and freedom. Consciously accepting their mortality and the fact that they have less control than they like to think over when and how they may die, they direct their energies less toward self-preservation and more toward living well in the present. They value life too much to take foolish risks, but they live in a confident and care-free way denied to the majority of people who have not had the opportunity to face death squarely and successfully. This is the best possible outcome.

The worst off are those who can neither defend themselves against their anxiety by suppressing it, nor face it and accept it. Their life experience or genetic endowment may not have given them sufficient courage; or those around them may not have given them enough support and reassurance during the phase of heightened insecurity. They become prey to all the manifestations of chronic anxiety, particularly hypochondriasis or obsessionality. Their relatives continue to be over-protective, and the ensuing picture is one of a restricted life-style and often misery for all concerned. This syndrome is easier to prevent than to treat, a fact which underlines the importance of attention to the psychological aspects of rehabilitation following life-threatening illness.

Uncertain death and an unknown time when the question will be resolved

The predominant feature of this trajectory is uncertainty. Multiple sclerosis provides a good example. There could be just one episode and no further development of the disease for many years, or ever; or it could pursue a remitting course, the patient always expecting another exacerbation and never knowing when it will come. More rarely, it progresses steadily and the hoped-for remissions are short lived and only partial. Wishing to gain some control over this frighteningly unpredictable state of affairs, the patient scans his life-style to see if he can pick out any pattern of precipitating factors that he could avoid in the future. He also investigates all sorts of possibilities that might offer a cure, and he supports research. In moderation, all this activity is constructive. Carried to excess, it leads to a preoccupation with the self and the illness which has a deleterious effect. This is because discomfort and misery thrive on attention and recede into the background when the patient can be deeply engrossed in other things. Accepting that he will nearly always have some symptoms, the doctor and patient need to work together to achieve the right balance between attending to them and ignoring them.

The cancer patient who has treatment which was intended, and indeed expected, to cure him also has to cope with uncertainty. Most people, but not all, know that if they have once had cancer there is always the possibility of recurrence. If a cure is very likely, there is no point in enlightening an unsuspecting patient and making him unnecessarily anxious. If he wants to know, he will draw conclusions from the fact that he is recalled regularly for follow-up examinations even though he

feels perfectly well. Patients often try to estimate the risk of
recurrence as much from the timing of follow-up appointments as
they do from clinical information given to them. Once they are
told that they need not come up for a year, they assume the risk is
negligible.

The anxiety level is highest soon after diagnosis and initial
treatment, and symptoms, from whatever cause, are seen as
possible signs of recurrence. The longer a patient remains
symptom free, the less anxious he becomes, although he may have
a painful resurgence of fear if a patient he knows becomes more ill
or dies, especially if both have the same form of cancer. When
there is an interval of many years before the first recurrence, the
patient often reacts with shock and also anger like someone totally
unprepared. He behaves as if he believes that his cancer, once
conquered, should not be able to creep up on him surreptitiously
and attack him again.

Someone who has had a heart attack or stroke responds initially
in the same way as to an accident. In addition he has to cope with
the knowledge that he may have another one at any time and that
one could prove fatal. If he realises that he might have died, he goes
through the experiences described in the preceding section. The
most favourable outcome is also similar: the patient accepts the
possibility of unexpected sudden death and does not let it interfere
unduly with his life-style. Over-use of the defence of denial is a
disadvantage in these patients as they may fail to heed advice given
to them about exertion or smoking. Eager to prove to themselves
and others that they are not worried, they may ignore premoni-
tory symptoms or even drive themselves harder than before, and
so increase the risk of a further attack. Again, those who can
neither defend themselves against anxiety nor accept the risk of
death do badly. Unless they are helped by a good rehabilitation
programme, they become disabled by long-term anxiety or
depression with many somatic symptoms such as chest pain and
breathlessness. Their family may share their anxiety, becoming
restricting and over-protective. However, if they sense that the
patient's problems are partly neurotic, they may resent his illness
and the limitations it imposes on them, becoming irritable or even
withdrawing from him and ignoring his complaints. If he then has
a further attack, the family reproach themselves for not taking him
seriously enough. Should he die, guilt may play a larger than usual
part in their response to bereavement.

References

1. Pattison E.M. (1977). *The Experience of Dying*, p. 47. London: Prentice-Hall.
2. Glaser B.G., Straus A.L. (1966). *Awareness of Dying*. Chicago: Aldine.
3. Glaser B.G., Straus A.L. (1968). *Time for Dying*. Chicago: Aldine.
4. Moody R.A. (1975). *Life After Life*. Georgia: Mocking Bird Books.
5. Kubler-Ross E. (1969). *On Death and Dying*. London: Macmillan.

6

Psychological responses to physical symptoms

There is a complex relationship between physical and psychological symptoms. When symptoms such as pain or nausea are not relieved by measures that are usually effective, the physician may suspect that underlying psychological problems are exacerbating or even provoking them. Such cases will be discussed in Chapter 13. Here, we are concerned with those situations in which the physical symptoms occur first and the psychological problems are a response to them.

Pain

The psychological reactions to pain are determined by a number of variables. The statement that acute pain is associated with anxiety, and chronic pain with depression is rather a crude generalisation, but it contains some truth. The severity of the concomitant anxiety or depression depends partly on the meaning of the pain for the patient. Thus a chest pain which the patient associates with indigestion is unlikely to provoke much anxiety (unless a relative of his died of a perforated ulcer), but a similar pain which he suspects is caused by heart disease may make him very anxious. Even severe pain can be tolerated for a short time if the patient knows that it does not have serious long-term implications and that it can be relieved in the foreseeable future. Patients who know they have cancer suspect that every new pain is evidence of recurrence, and are consequently made anxious by almost any pain, whatever its cause.

Chronic pain demoralises a person. It fills his world so that he cannot concentrate, and nothing can distract his attention from it. He sleeps badly and gets worn out. If he is one of those who believes that he should be able to ignore pain and 'soldier on', he will be ashamed of the way it has caused him to limit his life. If, in addition, he suspects that the failure of the doctors to relieve it means it has an untreatable or progressive cause, he will become even more depressed.

Essential to the management of these patients is accurate diagnosis of the cause of the pain, and the use of appropriate drugs or other measures to control it. When this is combined with discussion about the significance of the pain, the proposed method of treatment, and ways in which the patient himself can co-operate, relief of the primary symptom and its concomitants usually follows. Only if this fails, or there is obviously independent psychopathology, should a psychological cause be sought. Some patients suffer unnecessarily because pain from an organic lesion is assumed to be psychological, and others who have psychogenic pain suffer needlessly from over-investigation. The clinician only learns how to steer his way between these two through experience.

Anorexia

Anorexia is a symptom that worries some patients and relatives more than it should. Most people believe that death will follow quickly if they do not eat, despite what they probably know about the way prisoners on hunger strike live for many weeks. The patient who is aware that he is going to die in the near future, and that eating makes him uncomfortable, may be content to take just a little, if and when he fancies it. He is grateful when those around him find this acceptable. Sometimes relatives do not understand or have not reached the same level of acceptance. They make great efforts to encourage him to eat, bring him delicacies or insist on feeding him when he is very weak and would rather rest. They need help to realise that he is not being neglected if he is not fed, and that they can best express their love at this stage by leaving the choice to him.

Breathlessness

Breathlessness causes anxiety and is also exacerbated by it, so that it is very easy for a vicious circle to become established which is only broken when the patient can sleep. Yet sedatives have to be used cautiously because of the danger of respiratory depression. Patients with serious respiratory disease are often particularly afraid of death, suspecting that they will succumb while gasping and struggling to get their breath. They need to be given opportunities to talk through the fears that they have about dying, and to be reassured that drugs can and will be used when necessary to relieve their distress. Training in relaxation and breathing exercises may help them to gain control of that component of their breathlessness which is caused by anxiety. Then, instead of feeling ashamed that their worrying makes them worse, they gain some sense of mastery over their condition.

Weakness

When everything possible has been done to make a very ill patient comfortable, he may still be miserable because of feelings of overwhelming weakness, especially if he has always been independent and is ashamed that he now needs to have so much done for him. Not since childhood has someone else washed him, fed him, and attended to his most intimate needs. The idea that dependency is as natural toward the end of life as it is at the beginning may be new to him. If those around him accept this, he may do so too, and even begin to enjoy it. In hospital, nurses learn to encourage this kind of regression in the very ill, while maintaining their self-respect and dignity. At home a husband or wife may move into a parental role *vis-à-vis* the spouse. Done sensitively at the right time, it may bring out a tenderness which is mutually satisfying and helps to ease the pain of impending separation.

Boredom

Many very ill patients sleep for much of the day when there is nothing happening. Those who cannot sleep often become very bored. They cannot concentrate for long enough to read or enjoy television; poor sight or lack of co-ordination may make the simplest diversional activities impossible. Denied these helpful distractions, their tedious day may be filled with an incoherent jumble of memories and fears. Some patients like this cannot concentrate long enough to talk through these fears or accept reassurance, and cannot tolerate more than a few hours of wakefulness in the day. Sedation which allows them to sleep for most of the time, but leaves them easily rousable when visitors come, is ideal for them.

Paralysis

Neurological conditions like motor neuron disease produce some of the problems of the very weak patient, long before death is near. Paralysis is an extremely frustrating condition and hard to come to terms with. Sometimes relatives mistakenly equate physical helplessness with psychological regression.

Jean and Ken had to cope with this problem. Jean found that as Ken became floppy and she had to care for him as a great oversized baby, she responded to him in a maternal way or as a nurse, rather than a wife. His mother did this too; sitting by his bed holding his hand. Within himself he still felt a man. His bearded face and his voice were those of a man, and he wondered why he could no longer elicit the responses he was accustomed to from women. This made him very depressed but he said nothing, feeling that he ought to be grateful for all the care he was being given. When I saw Ken and Jean together he was able to explain this, and she understood. She realised that she had moved into a nurse role partly in order to become detached: her way of coping with her grief that she had lost her husband as he used to be. But she had not lost him as fully as she suspected. She had stopped undressing in the bedroom where he could see her, thinking that this would only frustrate him, reminding him that he could no longer make love as he used to. He then assumed that she had stopped loving him, so he never asked her why she had changed her ways. When this misunderstanding was resolved, she went back to giving him his usual morning and evening 'show', to their mutual pleasure. The acknowledgement that each still wanted and admired the other was important to the self-esteem of them both.

Personality change

Because this section is dealing with psychological problems directly related to the physical disease process, it is appropriate here to consider personality change due to primary and secondary brain tumours. This occurred in 2 of the 41 research couples. In the early stages the patient may be aware that he is 'not himself' and be upset by this. If he knows his diagnosis, he will benefit from being told that it is his tumour that is causing him to be different, and that staff understand this and will not think any the less of him as a person if he has lapses. The management of such patients will be considered further in Chapter 14. Usually it is the relatives who suffer when personality change occurs. They may be very embarrassed by the alteration in character: the coarsening of behaviour, unaccustomed rudeness or aggression, disinhibited sexuality, messy or voracious eating habits. One wife was so ashamed when this happened to her husband that she concealed their problems for as long as possible. She discouraged visitors and became very depressed. His way of eating nauseated her so that she lost her appetite and consequently also lost weight. She lost her sense of perspective too and began to believe his criticisms and his hateful remarks. She was most relieved when I, guessing what might be going on, asked her direct questions about it. To nurse a patient like this when he is a stranger is not too difficult, but to care for him day and night when he looks like the husband you have always loved, but now behaves like a totally different person, is very stressful indeed. This condition is almost always an indication for admission to hospital.

Anger

Many patients, after the initial reactions of shock and disbelief, respond with anger to the realisation that they may soon die. Usually this is very understandable to those around, who often feel the same way and so help the patient to express it and come to terms with the apparent unfairness of what is happening. Occasionally the anger is severe and prolonged, particularly when there have been unfortunate experiences which led to delay in diagnosis or inadequate treatment. Such a patient may become preoccupied with going over what happened and thinking about what might have been. If it seems clear from independent evidence that his complaints are justified, it helps him when staff acknowledge that they too understand and share his feelings. When he has had plenty of opportunity to work through them, it may be appropriate to remind him that going on being angry is very exhausting and destructive, and that he would enjoy the rest of his life more if he could let it drop.

Free-floating anger is hard to cope with, and some people cannot easily accept its irrational nature. They think it is pointless to be angry about something if there is nothing they can do about it and no obvious person to blame. They attempt to suppress what they regard as childish, unreasonable, or unchristian feelings. But anger is not to be disposed of so easily. If the supression is successful, the patient often becomes depressed, as if it has been turned in on him and beaten him down. The management of depression will be dealt with in Chapter 13; it is sufficient here to say that for these patients simple psychotherapy aimed at encouraging the expression of anger is a quicker and more effective treatment than anti–depressant drugs.

Anger may also be displaced: it is expressed but the target is inappropriate. Instead of being angry about what the doctor has told him, the patient is angry with the doctor himself, criticising his technique and his treatment. He may find fault with the very best of nursing care, and nothing anyone does for him ever seems right. Often it is the family members who bear the brunt of this and they become perplexed, wondering what they have done to offend him so badly. If this behaviour continues, he may alienate them and make himself unpopular with staff and patients alike. Then when he says that everyone is turning against him he may be correct, not paranoid. After listening to his complaints, it may be possible to help him correct the displacement by saying something like 'You seem to be cross with a lot of people today. I guess that deep down the real problem is that you are very angry that you are so ill and may die, and that no one seems able to stop it happening.' He may agree, and then he should be helped to express these feelings more fully in words or tears. Alternatively, he may angrily deny the truth of the interpretation, only later realising it was correct and experiencing the raw rage against God or fate which he was previously avoiding. Once this happens he begins to relate normally again to those around him and everyone feels relieved. Recognising and treating displacement in this way is not usually difficult and can be very rewarding. Such simple therapy can be carried out by almost any professional person who has a good rapport with the patient and is sensitive to his needs. A wise friend or relative may intuitively do much the same.

Prolonged and destructive anger is only one of the responses to terminal illness which cause unnecessary suffering to dying patients and their families. Others include adjustment reactions, depression, anxiety, and paranoia, and these also can sometimes be treated equally simply. In other instances, more experience and the use of psychotropic drugs make treatment more effective. For a few, the expertise of the psychiatrist is required. Later chapters will be devoted to a fuller discussion of these topics.

7

Psychological problems associated with treatment

Treatment for life-threatening disease often involves mutilating operations such as mastectomy and colostomy for cancer, or amputation of a limb that is likely to become gangrenous due to vascular disease. Patients accept such operations as the lesser of two evils, but they carry high levels of psychological morbidity, as Maguire et al.[1] have shown. They studied mastectomy patients and controls with benign breast disease and followed them for at least a year after surgery. Twenty-five per cent of the operated patients suffered from anxiety or depression of a moderate or severe degree, warranting psychiatric treatment, and three of those who were severely depressed attempted suicide. Sexual difficulties were assessed in those patients who had a regular and enjoyable love life before surgery. Thirty-three per cent of mastectomy patients (and 8% of controls) had developed sexual problems, and almost a third of the affected mastectomy couples no longer made love at all. A proportion of these problems could be regarded as a response to the knowledge that the surgery had been for cancer and that cure was uncertain, but many of them were quite directly related to the mutilating effect of the operation. Patients could not bear to look at themselves in the mirror and they made sure their husbands never saw their scars either. From other work, we know that colostomy patients sometimes react similarly, the husband or wife refusing to look at the stoma or help in the care.

In the case of mastectomy patients, Maguire et al.[2] have shown that though this morbidity cannot be prevented by preoperative and immediate postoperative counselling, it does respond to treatment. At 12 to 18 months follow-up, 39% of controls had significant psychiatric morbidity. The corresponding figure for patients counselled and monitored by their research nurse was only 12%. Most of the control patients were not offered help because no one involved in their care recognised their problem and they themselves were reluctant to report it. Alertness on the part of hospital staff and general practitioners to these treatable conditions could contribute to a significant reduction in suffering for these people.

Among the patients admitted to our unit, many had made a good adjustment to the effects of their operation. Mastectomy patients spoke of the support they received from staff and, most importantly, from their partners. Several women described how their husbands had helped them by being able to look at the scar from the beginning, and sharing their concern about obtaining a satisfactory prosthesis. A little extra attention and reassurance about her attractiveness helps such a woman resume her sexual life soon after operation, and doing this contributes to her general feeling of normality and well-being.

The support of a spouse is also important in coming to terms with an artificial stoma. One man told me how reassuring his wife's matter-of-fact approach was in the bedroom and bathroom. He thought to himself, 'If it doesn't make much difference to her, I guess it need not bother me all that much either', and he quickly became unaware of it for most of the day.

For a few patients the story was different. One elderly man was very depressed. It had been generally assumed that this was his response to the knowledge that he had cancer, and that therefore nothing much could be done about it. Questioning revealed that although he could cope with his colostomy very well without any assistance, his wife found it so unnatural and disgusting that she would no longer sleep in the same bedroom. He felt lonely and rejected, and angry that she could not cope. Their relationship, which had been moderately happy before, deteriorated. At a time when they needed support from each other, they were far apart, and it was this rather than any response to the possibility of death that was the main cause of the depression.

When I interviewed the wife I discovered that she had had a very fastidious upbringing and regarded anything to do with excretion as dirty and taboo. Being childless, she had been denied the experience of nappies, which might have helped her to overcome this. She therefore regarded her response to the colostomy as natural and her husband's anger with her as inexplicable and unreasonable. Discussion with the couple enabled him to understand her difficulty better and to separate her intolerance of the colostomy from her other, much warmer feelings about him. Then he felt less rejected and their general relationship (and his depression) improved, although she still could not bring herself to sleep in the same bed.

Another couple had a similar problem during the weeks of convalescence, before the old man was able to care for his colostomy himself. His wife could not face it, but his daughter who lived nearby could and did. He made his appreciation of her evident. His wife then became jealous and feelings of mother – daughter rivalry which had long been buried reappeared. In retrospect it might have been wiser to use the district nurse, but no one thought of this reason for turning down the offer made by a caring daughter, especially when staff were busy. And if this consequence could have been foreseen, would it have been right to deny the old man and his daughter this intimacy before his death? It was precious to them, but it was costly to the wife, who felt rejected, and the daughter, who felt guilty that her mother was being hurt. The ghost of Oedipus is never laid it seems. Even at this late stage, the ideal therapist might have been able to help all three by working to strengthen the bond between the couple so that the daughter could be loved as daughter and not as rival. Then, after his death, the two women would have been able to mourn their loss together and comfort each other.

In my series the majority of those who still had problems related to surgery were mastectomy patients, some of whom had had their operation years before. When they discovered that we were interested in their emotional and sexual problems, and could help them, they were indignant that no one had thought to ask them about these difficulties before. By the time they came to us, most were also coping with the added insults of hair loss due to chemotherapy and/or moon face and weight gain due to steroids. While they recognised that these treatments were keeping them alive, they lamented their effects very much.

The women who suffered most had less secure marriages, and felt that they needed to remain sexually attractive if they were to hold the affection of their husbands. Where this was understood and the husband provided extra reassurance and support, the wives grieved over their changed appearance but did not doubt that they were loved. However, such women are very vulnerable to misunderstandings, especially if communication within the couple is not good. For instance, one husband thought that if he said nothing about his wife's mastectomy and disregarded its effects as much as possible, she would be relieved that it had not put him off, and would therefore cope better. In fact she took his attitude as evidence that he did not care about what had happened to her, and this was the beginning of an estrangement which developed into the full syndrome of morbid jealousy, causing great suffering to the whole family. The treatment of this problem will be discussed in Chapter 15.

Hair loss, even though a wig is provided, and Cushingoid appearance do cause considerable distress to men and women alike. They feel they are no longer themselves and are reluctant to go out, wondering how people they meet will respond to the change. One patient described her dismay when she returned part time to her old job as a doctor's receptionist, and some of the patients she knew actually failed to recognise her. It takes courage to go on with normal activities when incidents like that occur, and some patients withdraw, becoming depressed and lonely. In such cases, reduction of the drug may be appropriate even at the risk of shortening life.

Steroids are used in conditions other than cancer, leukaemia, and the lymphomas, and they may have direct and serious psychological side-effects. The euphoria they often produce is sometimes beneficial, though a few patients complain that they know that their new cheerfulness is not 'real'. The mood can move beyond this into hypomania or mania; alternatively, steroids can produce severe depression with suicidal risk or a paranoid reaction. The management of these conditions will be dealt with in subsequent chapters.

To maintain good control of the variety of symptoms of serious illness, a large number of drugs may have to be used, some in very high doses. This in itself sometimes produces problems. Patients think they ought not to need so much medicine, especially if they feel reasonably well on the regime. Careful explanation of what each drug is for often seems to help. Accepting a patient's refusal to take an analgesic, even when staff know he will be in pain as a result of its omission, may convince him that it is necessary. Discussing side-effects with him beforehand, and allowing him to share in the decisions about his management, lessens his feelings of loss of control. In those situations where full pain relief, at least initially, can only be obtained at the expense of alertness, some patients dislike drowsiness so much that they opt for a modicum of pain, and this choice should be respected.

When the co-operation of patients is not achieved through mutual understanding, some of them control their drug intake by making light of their pain when talking to staff, and thus being given less than they really need. Sometimes these patients give a more accurate account to relatives, and even ask them not to tell the doctors. It is therefore essential to assess pain by non-verbal cues as well as by what the patient says, and to try to bring out into the open any anxieties the patient may have about the effects of his medication. The fear of addiction has been mentioned already in Chapter 2; other patients suspect that analgesics may shorten their lives. Noting that some patients in their ward died within a few days of a certain drug being given, or the commencement of an injection regime, they fear that it was the treatment rather than the disease that hastened death. Such a belief may just be the response of a frightened patient whose knowledge is limited, or it may be the first indication of developing paranoia. Either way, tactful explanation and management are required if the patient is to die feeling secure with those who are caring for him, and free of pain.

Decisions about treatment

Six of the 41 patients in my research series (15%) needed help in making decisions about the continuation of chemotherapy or other treatments aimed at controlling the progress of their malignant disease. The therapies in question all had unpleasant side-effects, and at this stage it was recognised that although the benefits they were likely to bring could be considerable, they were also likely to be short lived. The question was therefore raised 'Is it time to stop, and give symptomatic treatment only?' In theory, the needs and wishes of the patient should be paramount in determining what happens in these cases, but in practice the needs of doctors and relatives sometimes influence decisions more than they should.

Some doctors see their role mainly as curers: men and women who save lives. They feel they should strive to do this to the very last. The death of their patient is seen as a failure, and a betrayal of his trust, to be delayed for as long as possible. Having helped him to fight the illness in the early stages, such doctors are slow to notice that he has now reached the point where he no longer wants to battle on. They find it hard to admit that their patient will die, and are not confident in the alternative, less active role: giving symptomatic treatment only, together with emotional support through the last stages of the patient's life. Their attitude leads some patients to agree to treatment because they fear the doctor's disapproval if they refuse. Others do not want to let him down. As one woman put it to me, 'I said yes because he seemed so keen for me to have it, but really I did want to stop.'

When the patient has accepted that death is inevitable, relatives may still feel very unwilling to let him go. They enquire about and suggest alternative treatments, want second opinions, and urge the patient not to give up. They are driven by their own need to know that they have done their best; that 'no stone has been left unturned' in their efforts to prolong the life of the person they love. Once the force of their need is fully acknowledged by the doctors, and the patient, they become better able to balance it against the patient's wish for peace and comfort toward the end of his life.

Patients themselves can have mixed motives for accepting or refusing treatment. It cannot be forced on someone who refuses, nor should it be withheld from the patient who insists on going on, even when benefit is doubtful and side-effects are severe, but it is right to explore with the patient what lies behind his decision.

Vera was married, with teenage children. She had breast cancer which was moderately responsive to treatment, and the radio-therapist thought she might stay reasonably well for several years. In out-patients, she told him that she did not want any more chemotherapy. She found the side-effects intolerable, she said, and she thought the illness should be allowed to take its course. Sensing that there was something unusual about this attitude, he asked me to see her. She spoke freely to me, and I found a multitude of problems. Vera's upbringing had taught her not to complain. This was the reason why she did not admit to the full extent of the side-effects she was suffering, which made her very ill for several days after she returned home. Her sickness and misery were hard for her and made the family unhappy as they watched.

She and her husband Tony did not get on well together. He saw the care of her elderly parents as a demanding burden. 'Now you are ill' he said 'I can't cope with them as well', and he refused to take her over for her weekly visit to do their shopping and help them. She was very attached to them and concerned, so Tony's attitude made her very unhappy. Tony and their son did not get on well either, and sometimes she was at her wits end, trying to keep the peace between them. As she spoke, she wept, and it was clear that she was depressed. In other circumstances she might have contemplated suicide, but refusal of treatment seemed to her an easier and much more acceptable way out.

I talked things over with Tony and we then had two sessions together trying to understand and improve the family problems. The radiotherapist agreed to postpone the decision about chemotherapy, to modify the regime slightly to diminish the side-effects, and to offer her a bed in hospital until they subsided if she later accepted treatment. When he saw her again in three weeks time she was feeling much better. She said she now wished to go on fighting her illness, at least until her daughter was old enough to look after herself.

When a patient insists on going ahead with treatment that is causing more suffering than the illness, and is unlikely to bring about remission, this should also be discussed carefully with him. He may be a fighter, determined to take any chance, however small, that might give him a few more months of life. Young patients in particular respond like this and they should be given full support in their struggle for survival. Sometimes, however, the patient is driven by fear of death rather than by a genuine wish to live. The common fears and misconceptions that patients have about dying will be described in the next chapter. When the patient knows that symptomatic treatment can make him comfortable and perhaps even able to go home for a week or two, he may opt for this rather than the alternative of staying in hospital, unable to enjoy his family, and feeling very ill from the effects of drugs which will at most only postpone his death.

A young woman with rapidly progressive melanomatosis, unusually unresponsive to treatment, still wanted the treatment to be continued. Her parents were distressed by her suffering and told us they wished she would give in. They dare not say this to her, however, as they were afraid she would misunderstand and think they were worn out by her illness and wished for her death. She, on the other hand, knew that her parents had always had high expectations of her. She had done exceptionally well at school, obtained a good degree, and now had an excellent job. She told me that she had never let them, or indeed anybody, down. She thought they would see her as lacking in courage if she gave in, and she was determined that they should be proud of her to the end. It came as a great relief to her to be told that they loved her so much that her comfort and peace mattered more than anything else.

Patients and relatives often feel uneasy about discussing these issues with the doctor who is in charge of treatment, fearing that in so doing they are questioning his judgement or competence. Another professional who has sufficient knowledge to understand the issues involved, but on whom the patient is not dependent for day-to-day care, has an important role to play here. He or she can listen to the pros and cons, ask pertinent questions, give or obtain more information, and act as a trusted spokesman. The GP, nurse, social worker, psychiatrist, or priest are all on occasion in the position to do this. Even if it means risking an accusation that they are interfering, they should approach the doctor concerned and explain the situation as they see it, in order that the patient's real wishes can be ascertained and fulfilled.

References

1. Maguire G.P., Lee E.G., Bevington D.J., Kuchemann C.S., Crabtree R.J., Cornell C.E. (1978). Psychiatric problems in the first year after mastectomy. *British Medical Journal*; 1:963–5.
2. Maguire G.P., Tate A., Brooke M., Thomas C., Sellwood R. (1980). The effect of counselling on the psychiatric morbidity associated with mastectomy. *British Medical Journal*; 2:1454–6.

8

Fears of dying

Every dying person I have known has been afraid at some stage in their last illness. Yet many of them think they are unusual in this, and they worry that they will be regarded as cowards when death approaches. Such people have often been brought up to over-value bravery and despise the frightened as weak and spineless. They have not understood that the truly courageous man may be as frightened as any other; what singles him out is his capacity to cope in spite of it, and not be overwhelmed.

Some religious people in particular are ashamed of their fear, and feel they are letting God and the Church down if they show it. Having been told that 'Perfect love casts out fear', they think their anxiety means that they have not accepted God's love or trusted him enough, and they feel guilty. To them I sometimes say 'God gave you a fear of death as part of your equipment for living. It is the other side of your life instinct. It ensures that you look after yourself properly and do not take unnecessary risks. And if he gave it to you, he understands it. He will help you when you are afraid, and he does not want you to be ashamed.'

This *biological fear* is strongest in the young; in those who have had a short illness, and those who feel they have a lot of living left to do. For them it may be not so much fear as a reluctance to die, and anger that death is coming too soon. It does not disappear when it is understood and accepted, but it loses much of its power. It comes in waves like the pangs of grief, and people learn to ask for the reassurance of company when it appears. They become able to distance themselves from it a little, saying 'I have got the fear again' much as they might report a pain. The calming effects of morphine and diamorphine may prevent it somewhat in patients receiving these for pain. A small dose of diazepam or clobazam may help too, though some patients would rather be fully aware and cope with it with their own inner resources, or the help of a friend. When they first experience this fear, some people imagine it will escalate and that they will die in terror. In fact it usually becomes less of a problem as death approaches and the life instinct bows to its fate.

We all fear the *unknown*. For this reason too it is natural to fear dying. The many stories told by patients who nearly died (as already noted in Chapter 5) provide reassurance for a growing number of people. However, the sceptics will always point out that these patients did not actually die. We cannot ever be certain, as Jenny (of Chapter 4) said to me:

> 'I was very frightened when I first heard what I had got, although I suppose most people are frightened about dying and wonder what it is going to be like; and no one can tell, you know.'

I asked if she was still frightened:

> 'Not frightened, I don't think. In fact this morning when I was at home and felt so lousy I wished I was here [in the hospice, she meant]. In a funny way I thought of this as home. Well, if this is the place where you feel safe and looked after when you are poorly then this is natural I should think.'

I asked her if she had been much troubled by fear:

> 'No. It is just my own thing you know, the only thing I can think about all by myself. Everything else I have been able to share. It is the only thing that is just me; the only thing I have to do alone.'

Separation anxiety

Attachment theory, derived from the study of animals and young children, shows how the threat of separation from a parent figure provokes anxiety and awakens the primitive urge to cling to that figure. If the parent is not available, any familiar person helps. Research with children left in nursery schools shows that even the presence of a very young brother or sister allays anxiety considerably. Although adults are less dependent than children, they still form strong attachments, and at times of stress they want to be in close contact with those they love. The threat of death causes an upsurge of separation anxiety, and we know from experience that (provided there is not unrelieved physical distress) the presence of a close relative does more to bring peace to a dying person than any other measure. For this reason we sometimes put such a patient in a single room and provide an extra bed so that the spouse or parent can sleep nearby. Then both patient and relative rest more peacefully than they would if separated.

Existential fear

The existential fear of death, of ceasing to be, lies deep in everyone and usually remains unconscious. Its presence profoundly influences people's behaviour as the knowledge of death becomes inescapable in terminal illness, and the next chapter is about the various ways in which the psyche copes with this crisis. Most people never really believe even in the possibility that they could cease to be. The rare few who have talked to me about it, and who do seem to believe that death is the end, approach it in a calm and philosophical way. If they are going to be 'switched out like a light', as one patient put it to me, they see no future to fear. They may be angry that their lives are going to end prematurely, but they are not afraid.

It is almost impossible to imagine one's *self* dead; in any attempt one becomes a spectator of the scene, still somewhere around watching, or else departing off to another life. This inability to imagine being dead may be behind the fear of cremation that some people have. They are not confident that they will not feel the heat of the furnace. Likewise, a few fear burial, and both groups may be afraid that they will be certified as dead when it is not actually so. Such fears are reinforced by occasional reports of patients in very deep coma (usually people who have taken large over-doses of drugs) who are mistakenly taken to a mortuary, where they are observed to be breathing or to stir. Patients who have reached that depth of unconsciousness in fact rarely lighten much, or even survive unconscious for long. Fears of this kind occur earlier in the illness when the patient is still coming to terms with death. Later, when he knows from changes in his own body and feelings that he is dying, and he trusts those who are caring for him, they subside.

Fear of illness and dying

Fears about the process of dying cause more obvious suffering than the fear of death itself. Patients' ideas of what dying will be like sometimes originate from their memories of the death of a close relative or friend. If that was painful or frightening, they tend to assume all deaths are likely to be similar, especially if they are from the same disease. It is therefore wise to ask the patient what experiences of death he has already had. After he has told his story, he can often be reassured that his problems are different from those he has just described, or that methods of symptom relief have advanced so much that there is certainly no reason why he should suffer as 'X' did. One advantage of nursing hospitalised dying patients in with others is that people can see for themselves that the dying are cared for with gentleness and concern, even when they are unconscious, and that they are usually at peace. As Jenny said: 'Everything seems to happen peacefully here. I know how you look after people, and that you never want anyone to be in pain.'

Fear of pain

The commonest fear of all is that dying will be painful. The phrase 'died in agony' seems to be impressed on people's minds, providing grounds for an expectation that is ill-founded. This was underlined for us when the local press reported that someone well known in the neighbourhood had battled courageously with the pain of cancer until he died. We happened to know that the last part of his life was quite free from pain. Such inaccurate reporting perpetuates the myth that all cancer deaths are likely to be painful, and so reinforces fear. Many patients are surprised to be told that a significant percentage of people who are dying, even of cancer, do not experience any pain at all.

Those who have had severe pain which has not been taken seriously or treated effectively have more reason to be afraid. Even when their pain has been fully controlled for some time, they tend to assume that as death approaches it is bound to get much worse, reducing them once again to a shaking wreck. They are glad to be told that in many patients pain diminishes toward the end of life. Their worst worry is that they will reach a stage where it will become unbearable and that they will lose control, an experience that would also be distressing for those close to them. It is not appropriate to promise anyone that they will be kept totally free from pain for the rest of their life, even though it is often possible to do this. Few people ask for such a promise. What they do want (and this we can give to them) is assurance that they will not be in severe pain for any length of time, and that they will never be left alone with it. Although they would like to remain alert, most agree that if a choice has to be made near the end, they would make freedom from pain their first priority, and accept the possibility that the necessary drugs may make them drowsy or even a little confused. As one man put it when talking over this issue with me, 'I do not want to squirm out of this life', and he certainly did not.

Loss of control

The process of dying involves progressive loss of control over one's life. Even though it is partly illusory, we like the feeling that we are in charge of what is happening to us and that we can choose what we will do and when. This becomes progressively eroded as a person is forced by his illness to give up his job, and then one by one the other activities that affirm him in his various roles. Each of these losses has to be mourned, but many people, especially if understood and supported by friends and family, adapt surprisingly well and do not lose their self-esteem. Allowing people to continue to make as many decisions about themselves as possible confirms their value and helps them to retain a sense of power. Thus a mother may want to make the shopping list for the family for a long time after she becomes unable to visit the shops; and father may want to know all about the repairs to his son's motorbike even though he can no longer go and look at it. As the freedom to choose becomes more restricted, the choice of what to wear or to eat, and when to have a bath becomes more important to some people, and this should be allowed for in their care. They are more easily accommodated at home. In hospital their routine should be made as flexible as is compatible with the needs of other patients.

More frightening than the loss of control of external events and the activities of others is the loss of control of bodily and mental functions. When this begins, patients may feel that they really are disintegrating. Those who have been most independent are more affected. Having made great efforts to cope all their lives, some of them despise themselves for what they see as failure of willpower. They may accept the idea that it is only their body that is gradually wearing out, and that their 'real self' is as intact as ever and just as respected. Sometimes the great distress that patients experience when they become incontinent or messy can be traced back to childhood, and doing this actually helps them. Rather diffidently I tried this with a lady of 70 who was horrified when she wet the bed. 'I wonder' I said 'whether you feel embarrassed and expect the nurses to be angry because the last time you did this was when you were a little girl. It probably made your mother very cross, and you ashamed. Perhaps that memory, locked away for a lifetime, has something to do with how you feel now.' She was thoughtful for a moment. 'Maybe so' she said. The next time I was talking with the nurses about her they told me that she now accepted her occasional incontinence without shame, and could simply thank them for making her comfortable again.

Worst of all is the feeling of impending insanity – the ultimate in loss of control. Early dementia, hallucinations, and episodes of odd behaviour at night, all frighten some people into thinking they are about to go mad. I have known some patients try to hide these symptoms, fearing that they may be transferred to a psychiatric hospital. The management of these patients will be fully discussed in Chapter 10. Here it is sufficient to say that I have found the fear of insanity to be so common that I now ask about it routinely in any patient who has a condition that could possibly evoke it. 'Some people,' I may say, 'begin to wonder if they are going mad when things like this happen to them. Do you ever worry about this?' If the answer is in the negative, I can tell them how glad I am that they have not been troubled by such an unnecessary fear. Much more often the answer is 'Yes', and they are relieved that I have anticipated their worry and am willing to talk about it. They appreciate being told that we have met such problems before and that they are usually caused by the illness or by the drugs that are being used. Often something can be done to relieve them. If not, the assurance that we know that the patient *himself* is all right, even though his illness may make him do or experience unusual things, seems to remove any stigma associated with insanity, and so eases much of the concomitant distress in patients and relatives alike.

Fear of sudden death

On rare occasions, for example when a rapidly spreading cancer threatens to erode a major blood vessel, the fear of sudden death is well founded. The few patients like this that I have seen seemed unaware of their precarious state, and their activities were limited only by their general health. More common is an unrealistic and sometimes crippling fear of sudden death, occurring early in the illness when the diagnosis has recently been made, or a new symptom has developed. This is part of an anxiety state and sometimes is the cause of a kind of insomnia which is difficult to treat with sedatives. The patient suspects that he is more likely to die at night, when there are few people about and any sudden worsening of his condition might go unnoticed. (He may also be frightened to be left alone during the day.) He does his utmost to stay awake until dawn, and then drops off to sleep in the early morning. When asked about this pattern, he may acknowledge his fear, and that he feels safer asleep in daylight. If his previous questions and anxieties have been dealt with honestly, so that he trusts the staff, he usually accepts the assurance that none of us is expecting him to die in the near future. A small dose of diazepam may help him too. If he asks for a promise that he will be told if anything new causes us to revise our opinion, this assurance should be given. In practice he often recognises a change for himself when the time comes, and by then he is more prepared, so the person who keeps the promise is likely to get the quiet response, 'Yes, I thought so too'.

Fear of rejection

Patients whose illness causes disfigurement, a foul smell, or a marked change in appearance as does cachexia, sometimes refuse to see their families, and then become lonely and depressed. Of these, some genuinely wish to spare their relatives, and particularly children, the distress of seeing them as they are now. They may wish to be remembered as they were and fear that the shock of seeing them so ill will somehow wipe out the good memories. They need to be reassured that this will not be so. Where relatives have visited regularly and the progress of the disease has been gradual, they are saddened by it, but not repelled, but someone who has not visited for a long time will need to be prepared for the change.

Others refuse to see their families because they expect to be rejected and they would rather take this initiative than risk such a thing happening to them. If it is clear that the relatives are still prepared to visit, the patient should be gently helped to recognise that he is still loved and wanted. Often he can acknowledge that if the situation were reversed, he would on no account want to withdraw. Then he realises that both parties continue to lose out if he persists with his ban. Families who do find it hard to stay with a relative for these reasons need sympathy and support as they come to terms with the change in the person they love. They too benefit from reassurance that eventually they will be able to recall him fit and happy as he was before it all began.

Fear that cancer is contagious

Despite the general increase in knowledge about cancer, there is still a significant number of patients who believe that it is contagious. They may not speak about this, but may withdraw from their family because of their fear, becoming isolated and consequently depressed. I know of patients who have denied themselves a whole range of intimate contacts, from the kiss of a grandchild to sexual intercourse, in the belief that they would infect others. One lady who lived alone stopped inviting anyone in for a cup of tea or a meal, believing that her cancer could also be carried by crockery. Sometimes such a belief is part of a depressive illness and needs to be treated as such, but more often it is amenable to simple reassurance. The important thing is to think of it and ask the right questions; otherwise it may never be discovered at all.

As with any other fears, those associated with death and dying become much more tolerable once they have been shared. It is our responsibility to create an atmosphere which makes it as easy as possible for our patients to do this.

9

The fear of death and the journey to acceptance

Fear seems to be the first emotion a human being can express. A baby can be startled as soon as he is born, but it is several weeks before he can smile. I wonder if our knowledge of our own mortality is innate; present from the beginning, but unconscious. Maturation through childhood brings the means to conceptualise and communicate it. Then perhaps it is not so much that our experiences teach us about death; rather, they confront our defences against acknowledging its inevitability, and they allow awareness of this, with its attendant anxiety, to enter consciousness.

Developing awareness, and acceptance in old age

Intellectually everyone knows, at least from somewhere in middle childhood, that they will one day die. Yet it seems that everyone assumes that they will live to be old. This assumption too is usually unconscious, and shows its presence in the sense of outrage most people feel when suddenly confronted with the possibility that they will die 'prematurely'. Then they say 'But I was looking forward to . . . leaving school, getting married, having children, enjoying retirement, going to my grandchild's christening,' etc. For most people, the coming of death is bound to be 'too soon', and they feel robbed of the longevity which they took to be their birth-right. This response is strongest in the young, and gradually wanes as life tasks are completed, strength fails, and close relatives or friends die. The person who can look back on his life with satisfaction, knowing that on the whole he has done well, does not feel so strongly that he needs more time in which to develop unfulfilled potential, or to make amends. He can see old age as a bonus, a time of less responsibility and rush, when he can take each day as it comes. For him, death is not so threatening. He sees it more as a natural event, to mark the completion of his life. He may also be looking forward to eternity, to joining those who have 'gone before', to discovering what lies 'on the other side'. For such a person, death may come easily, as it should. Mortality is less alien for him, for he has had plenty of time and opportunity to accept its gradual approach as his life has progressed.

Existential denial

Along with the assumption that 'I will live to be old', most people also assume that death happens to other people, and only to them when they are old. Although they know from their television screen that appalling accidents happen, that people die in wars, and of starvation and disease, this all seems remote. Even more remote seems the possibility of nuclear war, despite the efforts of politicians and others to persuade them that it could really happen. Constant acute awareness of all these dangers would produce a state of paralysing anxiety, making daily living almost impossible. We need to be defended against this in order to survive, and this defence has been called existential denial. We can only cross the road, travel abroad, or plan for our future without undue fear because we have learned to live as if the dangers just described cannot touch us. (One way of understanding the phobic anxiety states is to regard them as conditions in which this defence of existential denial has broken down.)

First steps toward acceptance

For most people, the possibility of their own death remains remote until someone they know dies. Then they cannot escape the recognition that it happens to real people, even members of their own families. Provided the deceased is old, the threat still seems distant enough for personal safety, but should a contemporary – a sibling, school-friend, or workmate – die, the knowledge that 'I too might die' becomes inescapable and the process of assimilating this begins. Anger that such things can happen and grief for the death of the friend are coupled with similar feelings about one's own mortality. Anxiety rises for a time, and the person may respond by taking fewer risks, having a medical check-up, making a will, or investing in life insurance. Anxiety and grief then subside and life goes on much as before. A serious illness or an accident that was a 'close shave' brings the reality of death nearer still. The whole incident may provoke intolerable anxiety, and the memory of it be suppressed as effectively as the person's defence mechanisms allow; or it may be faced and worked through. Although this process is very stressful, the result can be a change in outlook and values which is salutary. Gratitude for survival, coupled with an acceptance that the future is uncertain, enables some people to make the most of each day as it comes, without spoiling it by undue concern with what tomorrow may bring. Such people have said to me 'You know, in an odd sort of way I am glad it happened, even though it was so awful at the time.' Part of the reason for their gladness is that they have faced their own death, and lost some of their fear of it.

The crisis of knowledge

Acceptance is a very gradual process, and it is only with increasing recognition of the certainty of death that the crisis comes (Fig. 9.1). If this occurs suddenly, either through accident or acute illness, or because psychological defences have prevented the realisation of the meaning of a slowly progressive disease, the first response is one of shock. Like the journey described in *Pilgrim's Progress* which Christian took to the Celestial City, the road from this initial shock to full acceptance has many side turnings and possible detours, and by no means everyone reaches the end. In this chapter I will only signpost the turnings as we pass, indicating the diagnostic destinations to which they lead. In later chapters their meaning and management will be discussed.

Usually the stage of shock soon passes into denial. To deny something vigorously is in itself an indication of awareness that it could be true, and must be defended against. For a rare few, even this is totally unacceptable. In rejecting it they temporarily lose their reason too, and suffer from a *psychogenic psychosis* (paranoia, psychotic depression, mania). Others cope in a different way. They banish from consciousness their knowledge that they are

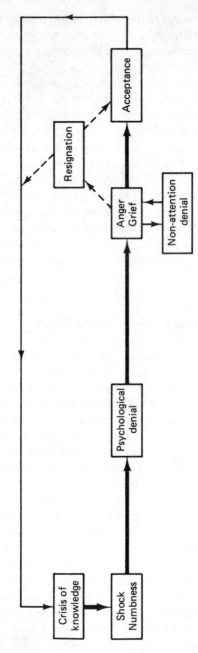

Fig. 9.1 The route from the crisis of knowledge to acceptance (modified from Kubler-Ross[1]).

likely to die, and they are not anxious. Instead they show the placid indifference of *conversion hysteria*, but they pay for this 'peace' by suffering from some disabling physical symptom such as paralysis.

Denial

The great majority are not diverted in these ways. In the throes of denial they say 'It can't be true; it isn't happening to me; there must be some mistake'. Some remain here for a time, using this defence (which Pattison[2] called psychological denial) to prevent them experiencing the anxiety that would accompany a fuller recognition of the truth. Doing this allows acceptance to come more gradually, and often such patients show evidence (through behaviour such as making a will or altering their plans for the future) that they have begun to take the new information into account, although they are not yet ready to talk about it. Eventually they abandon this stance, and I believe this defence should be respected and left alone for as long as the patient is coping well, accepting essential treatment, and is not disabled by anxiety. If *severe anxiety* breaks through, we know that the defence is no longer serving its purpose. Although the patient says he is not worried, he looks anxious, is restless and clinging, and his sleep may be disturbed by terrifying dreams or nightmares. To be effective, treatment may have to include confrontation of the denial as well as the use of anxiolytics.

Another detour leads to the destination of *somatic symptoms*, most often pain. The patient continues to deny that anything serious is wrong, and says that if only the pain could be relieved he would be all right. But, however skilfully the analgesics are manipulated or nerve blocks given, nothing brings relief, for his preoccupation with pain is enabling him to ignore his deeper anxieties. Again only treatment which will help him to face these and come to terms with them will afford lasting relief.

Anger, grief, and acceptance

As denial is abandoned, anger about what is happening and grief for what is being lost take over. This may happen repeatedly in a long illness. With each new loss or increase in disability (e.g. losing the status of wage-earner, recognition of the need for a wheelchair), there is an upsurge of anger and a period of mourning until adjustment is made to the new limitations, and new sources of satisfaction are found. Sometimes values change in a creative way.

> Mrs N. was a very particular housewife who felt she should clean her home every day. She did not entertain often for it was such an effort; everything had to be homemade and to a high standard. When she realised she might only have a few more months to live, she thought things out and altered her ways. On sunny mornings she would go out in the garden straight after breakfast, making the most of the good weather while she could, however dusty her house might be. Before, she entertained her grandchildren once a week to a meticulously prepared spread. Now she wanted to see as much of them as possible, and they came three times a week, ate bought cakes, and everyone enjoyed themselves immensely, for she had become more relaxed, more interested in them, and less in her own performance as a hostess and grandmother. Later, as her illness progressed and she could do less, she had fewer regrets and more good memories than she might have had, to occupy her mind when she could no longer be active.

Goals change too. In the early stages, they are more distant: to stay reasonably well for a daughter's wedding; to complete a task; to reach another birthday or anniversary. Each achievement brings satisfaction and the setting of a new goal. The recognition that some will never be reached brings with it not only new grief, but the setting of more limited objectives: to go home next weekend, to be awake and in the chair when the visitors come. Thus at every stage the sadness can be intermingled with contentment and even joy.

Non-attention denial

Not everyone who 'dies well' copes by steady step-wise acceptance. Some employ a strategy which Pattison[2] has called non-attention denial. Initially they recognise that they have an illness that could end in death. Often they face this with their family and they make essential financial and other arrangements.

Then they decide, more or less consciously, that they will live as if they are well for as long as possible. They behave as if their future prospects are unaffected by the illness, but it is interesting that some of them talk and plan, e.g. for a holiday abroad next year, but do not actually put down a deposit. In the short term, these people do not change their life-styles, and they may conceal their illness from almost everyone. Occasionally relatives who know of the serious prognosis wonder whether the patient has really understood, and they are uncertain how to respond to his cheerful talk about the future. More often they recognise and join in the game, agreeing with the patient's unspoken decision that the present must not be darkened by the shadow of the future. This coping strategy works well for many people, and they move into a phase of more open acceptance when concealment is no longer possible.

A few make a detour here and suffer unduly, through using the defence of *counter phobia*. They are so eager to prove to themselves and others that the illness is not affecting them that they try to do more than usual. They make a point of accepting challenges and may even take on extra commitments. This technique, 'ignore and fight', can be very effective. However, it can be carried too far, and then becomes counter-productive, resulting in exhaustion or a refusal to recognise further progress of the illness and seek renewed treatment or adequate analgesics.

Acceptance is not the same as resignation. It is a realistic appraisal of the situation as it changes, with a determination to adjust accordingly. In the early stages, many patients recognise that the odds are against them, but they choose to put up a fight. They obtain all the information they can about their condition and seek for themselves the best treatment they can find. They may supplement orthodox medical care with special diets, meditation, faith healing, etc., and may benefit from realising that they can contribute to the control of their condition and even strive for a cure. Meeting with other patients in an encouraging group atmosphere combats feelings of isolation or stigma, and improves morale. Anything that promotes physical, psychological, and spiritual well-being is likely to be of some benefit. Yet despite all this, for some the illness progresses steadily. They have to accept that their fight against the disease is definitely going to be lost, and that the time has come to direct all their remaining energies to accomplishing those things most dear to them, and to the giving and receiving of as much joy as possible in the time that is left. Eventually acceptance means giving up the fight altogether, relinquishing much-loved independence and entrusting themselves to others. At this stage they see no shame in regression to the physical helplessness of childhood, and are able to take pleasure in receiving attention and care.

However effectively troublesome symptoms such as pain or nausea are controlled, for some there is no escape from the weariness and boredom that come toward the end of life. They do not want to sleep all day, but no longer have the energy or concentration to enjoy anything for long. Like someone all prepared for a journey, they have said their goodbyes and the time for departure has come. This can be a difficult phase for everyone. Some are content just to wait; others reach a stage when they look forward to the release that death brings. Their families sense that they have withdrawn into themselves. Most appreciate the quiet presence of relatives, but a few indicate that they would rather be alone, perhaps wanting to spare them a prolonged and tiring vigil. Many are unconscious for the last hours or even days, perhaps stirring a little when they are moved or turned, and probably aware of at least some of what is said to them, for hearing seems to be the last of the senses to be lost. Eventually breathing and heart beat cease and death has come.

Not all deaths are like this, of course. Some occur suddenly, or in sleep, without preceding illness. In others control of pain and distress is not fully achieved; sometimes due to lack of skill on the part of those who are caring for the patient, and occasionally because the nature of the illness makes the difficulties almost insurmountable. Severe mental distress may occur too, especially when the patient is young and there has been little time for preparation, insufficient emotional support has been offered, or the patient, because of his personality and background, cannot make use of the help that is available.

Figure 9.2 summarises the journey described in this chapter, together with many of the detours that patients make: mania and hysteria are rare; paranoia is seen quite often; depression and anxiety are common. Sadly, some patients die in these states, either because no one treats them, or because time is too short or the condition too intractable to respond. The next six chapters describe the diagnosis and treatment of these conditions, using many case studies to illustrate the various points.

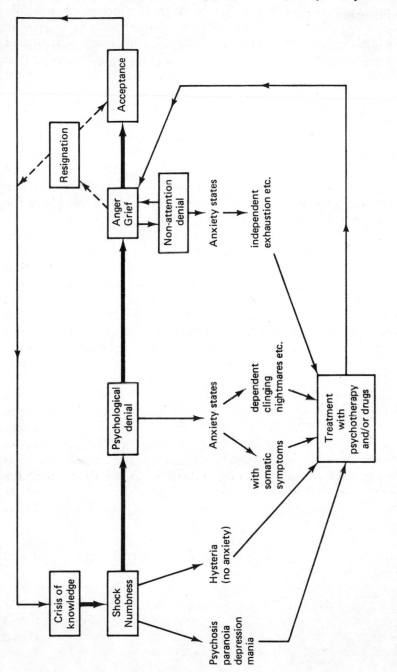

Fig. 9.2 Detours on the route.

References

1. Kubler-Ross E. (1969). *On Death and Dying*. London: Macmillan.
2. Pattison E.M. (1977). *The Experience of Dying*. London: Prentice-Hall.

10

Learning to adjust: problems involving communication and dependency

Some depression and anxiety is inevitable in anyone who is facing death. If either becomes severe or persistent, preventing the patient from living as well as he might in the circumstances, there is likely to be a treatable cause. In a few instances a diagnosis of anxiety state or depressive illness is appropriate. These will be considered in Chapters 12 and 13. More often the symptoms should be seen as indicative of unsolved problems, in the same way that a fever is usually indicative of infection. Treatment should be directed toward the problems themselves, and psychotropic drugs, like anti-pyretics in fever, are only needed if the agent provoking the symptoms cannot be dealt with directly, or the symptoms are so severe that they require treatment in their own right. The diagnostic label of 'adjustment reaction' (coding 309 in International Classification of Diseases[1]) fits the situation well. Adjustment reactions are described as 'mild or transient disorders . . . which occur in individuals of any age without pre-existing mental disorder'. They are often circumscribed, situation specific, generally reversible, and related in time and content to stresses such as separation experiences. Three main subgroups are noted: mainly depressive, mainly due to anxiety, or mainly a disturbance of conduct. The last is most commonly seen in children and adolescents.

Almost all patients admitted to our unit are anxious, not only because of their illness, but also (as in any other institution) because they have come to an unfamiliar place, to be cared for by strangers. Often they are uncertain about what treatment they will receive, and some are aware that they are unlikely ever to return home again. Most are sad too, for equally obvious reasons. As they become familiar with us and the routine, and symptoms such as pain or vomiting are brought under control, anxiety levels fall in the majority, and some of the sadness is also lost. For this reason patients are not referred to me for assessment of anxiety or depression until at least a few days have elapsed, unless their symptoms are very severe or were the main reason for admission in the first place.

There were 41 couples in my research project.[2,3] Among these, 29 patients were referred for a variety of reasons, and of the remaining 12, 2 were included because other members of staff thought they were coping exceptionally well, and 10 were chosen by our research nurse using a method designed to obtain a random selection of non-referred patients.

Table 10.1   Depression and anxiety in the research sample (percentages shown in brackets)

| | | Found on assessment | |
	Referred patients (n=29)	Referred patients (n=29)	Non-referred patients (n=12)	Total (n=41)
Depression	8 (28)	11 (38)	2 (17)	13 (32)
Anxiety	5 (17)	6 (21)	1 (8)	7 (17)

Table 10.1 shows the number of patients referred for depression and anxiety, and the number of cases found on assessment. Of the 13 patients whom I regarded as depressed (the diagnosis of depression in terminal illness will be discussed later), 2 were on anti-depressants at the time of admission, 2 were put on them later, and in 9 cases anti-depressants were not used at all. Of these 9, 6 improved following resolution of specific problems. Of the 3 who did not, one was very ill on admission and died within a few days, one had a brain tumour, and one had a 20-year history of chronic depression which had not responded to anti-depressants in the past. Of the 4 patients already on anti-depressants, 2 improved when problems were resolved, 1 improved dramatically in response to ECT, and 1 who had a long-standing marital problem which proved intractable, did not improve at all. So, in 8 of the 13 depressed patients, significant improvement in mood followed discussion and resolution of problems, and only in the patient who needed ECT was improvement directly related to anti-depressant treatment. (Among other patients, not in the research series, I have had a

few in whom psychotherapy alone was not effective and improvement did occur when anti-depressants were added.)

Unlike the depressed patients, all the anxious ones were already on an anxiolytic (usually diazepam) when I first saw them. This difference in prescribing tendency is probably due to the fact that terminally ill patients are often on analgesics which cause them to have a dry mouth, constipation, etc. Because the side-effects of anti-depressants make their problems worse, there is a reluctance to use them unless they are essential. Anxiolytics do not have these drawbacks, and are therefore used more freely. In the majority of anxious patients also, improvement seemed at least as much related to the resolution of problems as it was to increases in dosage of diazepam.

Adjustment reactions

Difficulties in adjustment arising in terminal illness can conveniently be discussed under four headings. The first two, communication and problems of dependency, will be dealt with in this chapter, and the third and fourth, adaptation to changes in role and the detrimental use of psychological defences, in the following one.

Communication

Communication has already been discussed at length in Chapters 3 and 4, but a few further points need to be made. It is generally assumed that people become more anxious when they are told that they have a terminal illness, but in a number of patients referred to me because of anxiety, their problem was that they had *not* been told. They were aware that they were becoming progressively more ill, and that different treatments had been tried but none had worked for long. People around them seemed very worried or unusually cheery and especially kind and considerate. They guessed that they were dying, but if they dared to ask questions, they got evasive answers or reassurances that did not ring true. They wanted to trust their families and the doctors, but could not ignore the insistent voice within them that said 'you are dying'. 'Is it true, or am I just getting depressed?' they wondered. Often such patients try to talk themselves out of their worry, but they do not succeed. They alternate between blaming themselves for being so pessimistic and thinking they are in the desperately lonely position of being the only person who knows the truth. They sense that those around them do not want them to ask, so they bear all this in solitude, but their expression and behaviour betray their increasing anxiety.

> Celia was one such patient. She had always been an anxious woman, and had a history of recurrent depression previously requiring psychiatric treatment. In view of this, her husband and her general practitioner agreed that it would be best to try to conceal the diagnosis from her for as long as possible. As she told me her story, it became clear that she was baffled by her lack of response to treatment, and very anxious indeed. Reluctantly and very sadly, for she was young and had only recently found happiness in a second marriage, I told her the diagnosis. In response to her direct questions, I indicated that I thought she only had weeks to live. 'That makes sense of so many things,' she said, and she told me how she had noticed changes in her husband's attitude, his reluctance to go ahead with long-term plans, and the fact that he now often seemed restless in his sleep. I had found the telling very hard, but as I rose to leave her she took my hand and said with a smile, 'Thank you for setting my mind at rest. Now I know what to do.' The next day her husband noticed a change in her expression as soon as he walked in. 'I know', she said, 'and I want us to go for a little holiday, to our favourite place, while there is still time.' The pain for which she was admitted became less and she seemed stronger, so she was discharged home a few days later. They took their holiday and enjoyed it very much. Soon after, she needed re-admission, but became well enough to go home for another weekend. Quite suddenly her condition deteriorated and there she died.

As has been discussed in the preceding chapter, a crisis of acute anxiety is common immediately after patients learn their diagnosis. In my experience, very few are made worse in the long term: among the couples in my study, there was only one – a man who persistently asked the home-care sister how ill he was and whether he was going to die. After stalling for some time, she told him the truth. Soon after that he started to have panic attacks, especially if his wife left him alone. These did not respond well to diazepam, but did improve considerably when his wife gave up her job so that she could spend more time with him.

Another patient, a man with carcinoma of the prostate, believed for a long time that his condition was benign. He had always suffered from muscular aches and pains, and once he knew the diagnosis he began to think that any new pain was a sign of spread of the cancer, so in this respect he became more anxious. For years his marriage had been unhappy and he had largely ignored his two sons. When he realised that he had a limited future, he took stock. He and his wife accepted marital therapy sessions with me, and he also discovered that his sons were more interesting and likeable than he had ever imagined. The day before he died, he told the nurse who was sitting with him how much he appreciated the changes we had helped him to make. Despite his intermittent anxiety, telling him the truth about his diagnosis did far more good than harm.

To depend or not to depend

The gradual transition from infancy to adulthood involves a change from dependency and helplessness toward independence and autonomy. As life moves toward its close, many people become progressively more helpless again, needing others to do for them those things that they had become so accustomed to doing for themselves. Most adults like to think of themselves as mature. Those who equate independence and autonomy with maturity will go on fighting to maintain these. Unconsciously they may still be like adolescents wanting to prove themselves, and to escape from over-protective parents. The fact that they now need care for quite different reasons seems irrelevant to them. They see the acceptance of help as 'giving in'; a regrettable weakness and a regression which for them is despicable. They are like the anxious but independent patients at the bottom of Fig. 9.2 who strive to convince themselves that they are not as ill as they really are, and who become exhausted by their efforts. Often they refuse adequate analgesia or further treatment. Their families watch them suffer, and they suffer too. Such patients may insist on living alone even when they have fallen several times, had accidents with the cooker, or started a fire. Some of them value independence so much that they would rather run the risk of dying alone than accept care, even though the chances are that their lives will be shorter and their end less comfortable.

Relatives of patients like this may need help to accept that they have a right to make their own decisions. Often there is some busy-body around who is ignorant of the facts and accuses the family of being negligent and uncaring, adding to their already painful sense of guilt.

When members of the family fail to persuade an ill person to accept care from them, or admission to hospital, an outsider may intervene successfully. The reason may lie in long-standing interpersonal difficulties within the family, and it may be impossible to do much about these. In such a case, increasing support from the community may be needed, in spite of the fact that relatives say that they are available. When the difficulty lies within the patient himself, simple psychotherapy may be effective. It involves helping him to see that maturity is not to be equated with independence, but includes a capacity to accept change and to respond to new situations in ways that bring most joy and least suffering to all concerned.

Some people have not realised that there is a natural change in the balance of dependence/independence through life. As children they are mainly dependent; in the middle years they are mainly active, giving and caring (in many instances to their own young children and their dependent parents). Toward the end it is again their turn to be mainly recipients. Not only do they need care now, they have earned it too. They have not stopped giving just because they are ill and inactive. They now have the chance to give their children the opportunity to care and serve; something that both can enjoy if the relationships are good. And they can still give interest, appreciation, and love. What the therapist is doing is giving the patient 'permission to regress'; to lose the shame he formerly associated with dependency and to enjoy his special position at the centre of the family, a place he probably has not held since he was a baby.

Regression, when it goes hand in hand with physical helplessness, can be a source of satisfaction to both patient and relatives (or nurses). The patient can enjoy having her hair combed and her face gently washed when she reaches the point where it would make her arms ache to do it for herself. The relatives who do these things can take pleasure in the new intimacy and in their own skill in giving physical comfort to the person they love. A good marriage relationship includes the capacity of the couple to parent each other at times of need. In terminal illness this part of the relationship may come to the fore, the patient becoming childlike and the spouse responding easily and naturally as parent. Provided it has been a reasonably secure marriage, both adapt well to this and it is to be encouraged.

Where the marriage bonds are less secure, the patient may turn to parents and reject the spouse. This can happen to a couple who are deeply in love but have not been married long. The patient has been used to turning to parents at times of weakness and fear, and has not had many opportunities to gain confidence in his or her partner's capacity to be supportive in a crisis. The young spouse feels hurt and rejected and needs help to understand that this regression is natural, and need not imply that he or she has failed to give enough love. Tactful parents will do their best to preserve the developing bond within the couple, but sometimes it is too tenuous to survive the stress of the threat of death. Then the spouse has to be helped to accept that the husband or wife is happier in the care of parents. One such husband reverted to his bachelor ways before his young wife died, and needed much support at the time of her death to help him with his anger that she had rejected him, and his guilt that he had then turned away from her.

The same sequence of events can occur when the marriage has been an unhappy one. If the parents of these patients have been possessive, and especially if they have disliked their in-law son or daughter and have not approved of the marriage, they may encourage the patient to turn to them and reject the spouse. Alternatively they may have good reason to suspect that the spouse will not rise to the occasion when needed. (I have seen marriages where terminal illness was 'the last straw' and the partner left the dying spouse soon after the diagnosis was known.) There are some really bad marriages with many problems on both sides, where the partners have stayed together 'for the sake of the children' or because they were too demoralised to do anything about separating. For these, terminal illness can be a release, and there may be relief for them both that nature has provided a parting. But most who are unhappy but who still stay together have been very ambivalent. Some couples like this do respond to marital therapy. Knowing that time is short, they make an effort to reach a new understanding, and use the time that is left to heal some of the mutual hurts. When this does happen, the patient dies more peacefully and the surviving spouse probably has less guilt to contend with during bereavement.

Earlier, 'permission to regress' was mentioned. Problems in adjustment can go the other way, with the patient becoming helpless and demanding when those around recognise that there are still many things he can do for himself. There are several reasons for this. A patient, either because of deprivation in early life, or because he has never grown out of being waited on by others, may use illness as a means of getting attention that he is too unlovable to obtain in other ways. When this happens, the family often feels manipulated, particularly if it is noticed that he can still do things he really wants to, and that he always manages to ask for help at the most inconvenient moment. If this is a long-standing pattern, exaggerated by illness, there is often little that can be done to change it, especially within the family. When patients like this come into hospital, some do alter after a while. A policy of being as generous and caring as possible, coupled with firmness at times when they compete unreasonably with others for attention, may win in the end. When they feel consistently valued and loved, they may become less demanding and even start to be appreciative. Helping the staff to understand them, and to cope with their own feelings of being 'put upon' is part of the management here.

Other patients become prematurely helpless to avoid being confronted with the signs of progress of their illness.

> Mr M. was referred because he seemed to be depressed. We knew he could walk short distances, but he insisted on sitting by his bed all day, complaining of being bored, and looking most unhappy. In a candid moment he explained, 'While I am sitting here I can imagine myself walking all the way down to the day room. Last time I tried it I was out of breath before I got half way. I don't want to try it again.' We talked about how painful it had been to discover his limitations; that it meant that he was getting worse, and that one day he might be too breathless to walk at all. This led on to a recognition that fear of the future was stopping him from enjoying the present, and that if he walked slowly, with rests, he could still get about wherever he wanted to, at least within the unit. A few days later he was in that day room, putting on his favourite record. Anti-depressants would not have done that; helping him to gain insight did.

References

1. *International Classification of Diseases, Injuries and Causes of Death: Mental Disorders Section*, 9th revision (1980). Copyright Wyeth 1980 from the World Health Organisation, Geneva.
2. Stedeford A. (1981). Couples facing death I – psychosocial aspects. *British Medical Journal*; **283**:1033 – 6.
3. Stedeford A. (1981). Couples facing death II – unsatisfactory communication. *British Medical Journal*; **283**:1098–1101.

I I

Adjusting to a changing role, and the detrimental use of psychological defences

Adjusting to changes in role

Changes in role and life-style are stressful. If too many occur too close together, even the ones that are chosen, like gaining promotion or getting married, have been shown to predispose people to depression. Enforced changes which are unwelcome and accompanied by ill-health are potentially much more harmful.

The emotional pain of losing an accustomed and valued role can be coped with adaptively, leading to a good outcome, or maladaptively, causing unnecessary suffering. A common situation which illustrates this problem is that where the husband in a couple is the only driver. If he becomes ill, his wife may decide she would like to learn to drive too. I saw three couples like this and their responses are instructive. All three men grieved that they could no longer drive. They disliked the idea of their wives taking over something that they had regarded as their prerogative, and which gave them pleasure. Two of the wives began to take lessons, and each was aware of her husband's mixed feelings about what she was doing. In one instance he made it so obvious that he was unhappy about it that she became unduly nervous and then discouraged. Finally she gave up, and blamed herself for being no good. The other husband saw that his wife needed encouragement, and that there would be obvious gains for them both if she passed her test. His resentment gave way to pride in her as she progressed. We shared their pleasure on the first day that she drove up alone to visit him, neatly parking the car where he could see it from his window. After that she could come more often and at times to suit herself, and she could also take him out. They both knew she was better prepared for widowhood as a result of her achievement.

The first husband was really more angry about his illness than he was about his wife driving his car. If he had been helped to recognise this, or his wife had been encouraged to persist and not to take his resentment so personally, the outcome might have been better. When a couple can share their anger against a common enemy, e.g. the threat of death, they are drawn together. The couple just described displaced it on to each other. He was angry with her for taking over his role, and she with him for being so discouraging, so they were being pushed apart.

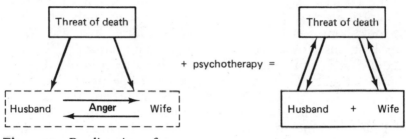

Fig. 11.1   Re–direction of anger.

Figure 11.1 depicts this diagrammatically. Sometimes I draw this during a consultation to help patients to understand what they are doing; saying to them: 'I think you are both most angry about the illness and anxious about what is going to happen. These are difficult things to talk about, but if you can manage to share some of the feelings and direct your anger where it belongs, you will stop taking it out on each other and probably feel a lot better.'

The third couple could not be helped at all. Here the husband's inability to tolerate the idea of his wife learning to drive was symptomatic of much deeper problems in the marriage. He was very insecure and boosted his self-esteem by maintaining control over everything he could, and making his wife feel useless and incompetent. Although she had long cherished a wish to drive, he was so upset at the idea (disguised as solicitous concern for her safety!) that she did not even begin. In bereavement, she was disabled by helplessness and anger at being abandoned by the man who had 'done everything for her' and so left her unduly dependent.

Vera and Tony (first mentioned in Chapter 7) had difficulty in adjusting their roles with regard to housework and the care of the children. Tony was very anxious when the consultant told him that Vera had cancer, and he did not take in what was said to him about prognosis. He assumed that she only had a short time left, and that she might feel better and live longer if he took over all her chores and allowed her to rest. Each morning he got up early to do some housework and see the children off to school. Previously he had sometimes come home from work to find her tired and tearful as she struggled to prepare the evening meal. Now he forbade her to do this, and she, being rather afraid of him, complied. She became depressed, complaining that she was no use to anyone and only a burden. It took Tony some time to realise that although he was doing his best, his efforts were making his wife unhappy. She felt redundant (a situation which would have been intolerable for him) and guilty because he now seemed to be always busy and tired. He had to accept her need to be useful and the fact that she might sometimes do too much and temporarily wear herself out. Once they achieved a better balance, she became less depressed and he less harassed.

Adaptation to the loss of the maternal role is illustrated by the next case.

> Daphne (Chapter 4) had been in hospital for several weeks before she was well enough to make a weekend visit home. While she was there, one of her children fell down and hurt his knee. As soon as he got up, he ran crying to his father for comfort. Naturally Daphne expected him to turn to her as he had always done in the past. She felt hurt, rejected, and angry with her little son. Had she remained in that mood, she would have become estranged from him and both would have missed out on the love they still had for each other. But she worked through her distress and said to me: 'I have realised that it is for the best that he is turning to his daddy now. It means that I don't have to worry about him so much when I am not there, and he won't miss me so much in the future.' She was accepting her diminishing role as a mother. Likewise, she told us of her husband's efforts at cooking. At first she resented his growing competence, but later she said, 'I never would have guessed he could do so well', and she became proud of him. Some people make these adjustments intuitively. Others need help to recognise and express their pain and resentment before they can move on toward acceptance.

Detrimental use of defences

We have already considered the way people use or misuse denial to enable them to cope with the knowledge of mortality. Other unacceptable thoughts or wishes, particularly those which might lead to intolerable anger or shame, are similarly defended against. Sometimes the use of these defences becomes counter-productive and the patient may benefit greatly from being helped to understand what he is doing.

> Mrs L. was a married woman in her forties with teenage children. She and her husband were rather particular about order and tidiness at home. As she became more ill, he busied himself incessantly in the evenings, doing what he felt was the essential housework which she could no longer do. He was too preoccupied with this to talk to her or to sit down with her. On Saturdays he made the children stay in to help and she overheard the shouting and grumbling that ensued. He could not understand her plea for peace and quiet, and in the end she asked to come into hospital, although from the point of view of her illness she could still have been nursed at home. She seemed unduly sleepy and admitted that sleep was her way of 'switching off'. Her husband visited only briefly, and tended to avoid the staff, as if he feared that a conversation might lead to something he could not cope with.

I helped her to understand how her husband was using over-activity and obsessionality as defences by asking her if he was the sort of person who tried to fend off anxiety by keeping very busy. She agreed that he was. I told her that I knew some people whose fear of an impending major change in their lives made them strive to keep everything around them just as it always used to be. She had seen her husband's behaviour as unkind and thoughtless, and even crazy, and had shouted at him that he needed a psychiatrist. Once she recognised that he was behaving like this because he was worried about her, she took a different attitude. Tactfully she persuaded him to talk with us and we helped him to face his fears and to understand his wife's unhappiness and need for quiet. Rather anxiously she agreed to go home for 24 hours and was surprised that she felt so much better there than before. The rushing around had ceased; friction between father and children diminished. Soon she asked to go home again, for a longer time. She became more alert, despite the fact that her illness was progressing, and we noted that her husband stayed with her longer and was much more at ease.

Mr R. used denial and displacement to the disadvantage of himself and his wife. He had been in the RAMC during the war and declared that he had got used to death then. 'I am not worried about what is going to happen to me,' he said (denial); 'I am only worried about my wife' (displacement). Most of the time he seemed cheerful and contented, but when she visited he was very anxious indeed. If she was a few minutes late, he was convinced that she had been involved in an accident, and when she arrived he scolded her for worrying him so much. He questioned her about everything she had done since he saw her last, and criticised much of what she told him. She disliked hospitals and illness anyway, and his unusual behaviour made her even more ill at ease. Her visits became briefer and more fraught, and he began to think she did not care about him. He was displacing his anxiety about himself on to her, and making her very unhappy. When we recognised this, I gently confronted him, saying that most people in his position *were* worried about themselves as well as their wives, and that I suspected that he was too. After vigorous denial he became upset and admitted that he had been trying not to think about the fact that he was dying. For two or three days his general level of anxiety rose; he demanded a lot of attention from the nurses and slept less well. But agitation over his wife's visits ceased. When she noticed the change she began to relax and stay longer. I helped them to talk together for the first time about his prognosis. Within a week she was spending many hours each day by his bedside. Her fear of hospitals had gone and she sat and knitted, quietly keeping him company as she might have done at home.

These two cases illustrate how the maladaptive use of defences against anxiety can lead to deteriorating relationships. If the people concerned had not been helped to reverse the process, it is likely that the antagonism would have continued. When this happens, rejection can occur, leading to anger, or to guilt and depression. If the couple were close before, one or both may sense that something is pushing them apart at a crucial time when they would normally be drawn together. Perplexed by this, they feel helpless in their estrangement. Fortunately one partner, more often the one who is not ill, eventually comes to realise that the patient is feeling thus in response to the illness, and not because of anything one or other has done. Then he or she can wait with more tolerance for the painful phase to be worked through, ready for reconciliation the moment it becomes possible. If this does not happen, and the patient dies while they are still estranged, the death is less likely to be peaceful and, in bereavement, the partner suffers unduly from guilt and regret.

Anger is as natural a response to terminal illness as anxiety. Maladaptive defences against this may lead to depression.

Mrs B., aged 53, was suffering from breast cancer and a secondary tumour was causing severe pain in her back and one leg. It was the type of pain usually relieved by a nerve block. This was done successfully, but within 24 hours she rapidly became paralysed from the waist down. Investigations showed that the cause was another metastasis which had led to the collapse of a vertebra higher up, compressing her spinal cord. She was devastated by this sudden worsening of her condition and listened in silence to the explanation about why it had come about. Depression supervened, accompanied by an unwillingness to adapt to her new situation. She was not in pain and could have got about well in a wheelchair and even been discharged home. But she refused to co-operate in efforts to rehabilitate her, remaining apathetic or irritable. Rather reluctantly she agreed to talk to me.

As I took her history I learned that she came from a family with undue respect for authority, where complaining was frowned on and the open expression of anger had never been allowed. As she became engrossed in her conversation with me, she admitted that she thought the doctor who did the nerve block had put the needle in the wrong place and had caused her paralysis. She became increasingly tense and began to be angry. I encouraged her in the latter, saying that anyone who had been through such a sequence of events might think the same. Suddenly she must have felt that she had gone too far, for she collected herself and changed the subject abruptly. I thought we had made a good start so I accepted her manoeuvre and let the matter rest there for that day.

After I left her, she complained that I had upset her terribly, and said that she would never see me again. I was not able to re-establish the rapport which we had initially achieved, presumably because she was both frightened and ashamed of the anger she had expressed and of her unaccustomed audacity in accusing a doctor of incompetence. Other members of staff were not successful in taking it up again either. After that one outburst she retreated, this time into more profound depression. Anti-depressants had no effect. Bored, and saying she was too ill to get up, she died slowly and miserably, leaving everyone around her feeling that they had failed.

If she could have continued to experience her anger, perhaps accusing to his face the doctor concerned, she might have come to terms with it. The energy which she had to use to suppress those feelings could then have been re-directed in a determination to live as well as she could in spite of her disability. But her background and personality meant that for her, depression was more acceptable than anger. At her age and with so little time available, she could not change.

Depression, related to suppressed anger, is most commonly seen in illnesses where there has been a delay in diagnosis. In malignant disease, I have encountered it most often with carcinoma of the pancreas. Here the onset is insidious, symptoms may be vague, and even the most careful investigations may not reveal any abnormality. The patient senses that he is seriously ill but his doctors, finding nothing physically wrong, tell him it must be 'nerves' and prescribe accordingly. The patient often oscillates between inner certainty that he is right, and shame that he cannot pull himself together if there is really nothing seriously wrong. This may go on for months or even a year or two before very severe pain, gross weight loss, or jaundice makes the diagnosis clear. Initially the patient feels relief that at last someone knows what the matter is, but this is usually followed by anger that the diagnosis was not made sooner, and that no curative treatment is possible. As this fact is accepted, the patient grieves. If, like Mrs B., he cannot cope with the anger, he is likely to become very depressed. Carcinoma of the pancreas is often associated with depression, particularly in these cases. Yet even here I have seen patients adjust well, responding to psychotherapy or anti-depressants, or both, or just coping through their own courage and resilience.

Psychotherapy of the kind described in this chapter can be offered by a number of professionals, and even on occasion by a wise and intuitive friend. If the helper understands the mechanisms involved and rapport is good, it may only need one or two interviews to bring about a change which benefits patient and family considerably. Medication may be required in addition, but it is seldom very effective while problems like these remain unsolved.

12

Anxiety

Terminal illness is usually accompanied by anxiety, but the illness is not necessarily the sole or main cause. The anxiety may be in response to problems in adjustment, which should always be looked for and treated where possible. Anxious patients, whether they have adjustment reactions or not, may belong to one of two groups: those with a high level of free-floating anxiety, often present for many years; and those who suffer from situational anxiety when exposed to specific stresses but who are able most of the time to 'take things in their stride'. These latter are usually much easier to treat.

When faced with a very anxious patient for whom treatment has little effect, the history that he or his family gives may reveal that he has 'always been like that'. Often there is a background of insecurity produced by, for example, traumatic experiences of separation or loss that have left the person constantly vigilant for any new threat. Sometimes he has dealt with previous crises, especially bereavement, by using denial or other defences instead of facing reality and working through the feelings that that evokes. When this is so, he lacks the confidence in his capacity to cope which is one of the gains from successful grieving.

Anxiety may present as complaints of subjective emotional distress ranging from a feeling of unease or threat right up to panic attacks when the patient may be terrified and think that he is going to faint or die immediately. As the diagram in Chapter 9 (Fig. 9.2) indicates, some patients deny that they are anxious, but their behaviour gives them away. They may suffer from frightening dreams or nightmares, or from insomnia. When awake they may be constantly active in a disorganised fashion, talkative, clinging, and demanding attention. Their expression is tense as is their posture; they sit on the edge of the chair or are unable to relax into their pillows in bed. Restlessly they watch all that is going on around them. They may make a great effort to remain independent and to prove to themselves that there is really nothing to worry about. For others the main expression of the anxiety is through physical symptoms such as pain, vomiting, or restlessness, which cannot be fully accounted for by the extent of the disease and which do not respond to levels of medication which would usually be adequate.

Separation anxiety

Many patients with chronic anxiety feel worse in unfamiliar surroundings and when separated from their family. Calling in a close relative to be with them often has a very calming effect. Frightened people need physical contact to reassure them, and a nurse who can sit quietly holding their hand or offering the kind of comfort one gives to a sick child may bring considerable relief. In cases where it is apparent that the presence of a relative is particularly helpful, we often encourage them to stay the night with the patient, moving him if possible into a single room and putting up a temporary bed beside his own. Both sleep more soundly in these circumstances. If the patient is likely to die in the next few days, the relative at home sleeps only fitfully, always listening for the telephone. In hospital he knows that he will be awakened as soon as he is needed, so he is no longer anxious about whether he will get there in time.

Insomnia

Some anxious patients are afraid to go to sleep because they have had unpleasant dreams or nightmares and dread their recurrence. The management of these will be discussed in the chapter on confusion (Chapter 14). Others stay awake all night because they are afraid of sudden death. This fear can be present early in the illness when it is not appropriate, and the patient does not reveal that he is 'fighting sleep' unless directly questioned. Then he may admit to thinking that in the hours of darkness his condition may worsen and no one will notice or do anything to resuscitate or rescue him. As soon as it is light and others are awake or busy around him, he feels it is safer to go to sleep. Coping with this problem is discussed in Chapter 8.

Pain

Pain may be the direct result of muscles being held tense in the posture of anxiety (as was the case with Françoise in Chapter 1). Tension headaches, pain in the neck, shoulders, arms and back are all common responses. When a movement is likely to be painful, for example because of a bony secondary deposit, or has been painful in the past before treatment, muscles go into spasm to avoid that movement and so produce a secondary pain. Diazepam often helps because it acts by relaxing such muscle spasm directly as well as relieving the anxiety. The posture of anxiety is partly habitual so that even when the cause is treated, it may persist. The physiotherapist or relaxation therapist may be able to offer effective treatment. She helps the patient to become more aware of his physical tension (which he often is not), shows him how to correct his posture, and teaches him to relax. She may use a tape which she has prepared for him, and which he can then use regularly when she is not there. Anxiety causes tension, but tension also causes anxiety, and learning to relax the body may also lead to a lessening of the emotional distress. The patient may be surprised and pleased to discover that there is something he can do for himself to relieve his pain. This sense of mastery increases his self-esteem at a time when the helplessness so often associated with the illness would otherwise get him down. When the therapist combines with the physical training the discussion of more positive mental attitudes, the overall effect may be very good. Introducing the interested patient to meditation or yoga may be beneficial, and reminding the music lover of the peace and pleasure to be gained from listening to his favourite tapes is well worth doing.

Pain may be used unconsciously by a patient as a means of adapting to a situation. This does not mean that he suffers less or that his pain is not 'real', but it does mean that the pain is resistant to treatment because relinquishing it necessitates facing the problem and coping with it in a different way. The three following case histories illustrate this.

> Mrs C. had surgery for cancer of the colon and seemed to be doing well, although it was known that she had metastases in her liver. She had lived alone in Scotland ever since her husband died. Six months after her operation she came south to spend a holiday with

her newly married son and his wife in their new home. While there, she developed abdominal pain which puzzled the GP and was not responsive to analgesics, so she was admitted for investigation. We too found the pain difficult to understand. Sometimes she would be very distressed by it, but by the time extra medication had been brought to her it had gone, and she wondered what the pill was for. On doctors' rounds she often said her pain was better, or gave a vague and variable description of it, but to her son and his wife she complained that it was agony and that we were doing very little to help her. Indeed she often did seem worse when they visited; when she went out to spend the day with them she had to come back prematurely because 'the pain made her so ill'.

When I saw her we talked about the future, and it became clear that she was afraid of returning home as she had few friends and did not find her local doctor and his team at all supportive. She knew she was welcome to be with her son for a holiday, but to stay with him for weeks or months seemed wrong. She felt that the couple needed to be alone in their new home together. To move into other accommodation nearby would not be acceptable to the son as he felt that if his mother was well enough to be discharged from hospital, he and his wife ought to look after her themselves; yet he knew his wife was reluctant to do this. The puzzling and persistent pain solved everyone's problem except ours. We would have liked to use her bed for a series of patients whose conditions were more responsive to treatment, but in the end we had to accept that her emotional and social problem was an insoluble one for her, and itself justified her continued stay. We hoped that by assuring her that she could remain with us as if we were her second home, she would be able to relinquish her pain and at least enjoy outings and visits with her son and daughter-in-law. But pain spoiled every trip, although she was often well on other days. She behaved as if pain was the price she paid for security with us, and she just could not afford to take the risk of losing it.

Peter had a bony tumour in his thigh which was painful and made his leg swollen and useless. It had already spread so that amputation would not have offered even a possibility of cure. He had a young wife and baby, but the marriage was unhappy and he guessed that while he was in hospital she was 'going around with one of his mates' and that the baby was being neglected. He came from a family with many social problems and his parents lacked the resources to support him through this tragedy. When first admitted he was preoccupied with pain, and nothing else seemed to matter. Gradually this came under control and symptoms of anxiety emerged more clearly. Then it seemed impossible to get him completely pain free. One day he said: 'Quite frankly, I miss the pain – it was awful but at least it took my mind off everything else.' He too needed his pain. His social worker worked intensively with his wife and family to try to help them. It wasn't until relationships improved and he had begun to come to terms with parting from his wife and child as well as losing his life, that the physical pain was fully relieved.

Other patients have said that a moderate degree of pain is more bearable than emotional distress. It is easier to complain about and attracts attention and sympathy in situations where others also cannot cope with the emotional problems. On occasion it allows anger to be displaced from its original causes onto the doctors, who become scapegoats, blamed for negligence and incompetence. One such relative said to me: 'I thought this place had a reputation for pain relief. You have been no use at all to my mother.' He could not accept our explanation of why this particular pain was so hard to treat, and we were left to bear his accusation.

In the third case pain was not a means of coping with anxiety but a way of expressing need, in a patient with a personality disorder. It is included here because we are considering cases where psychological problems perpetuate pain or interfere with its relief.

Mrs N. (Chapter 9) was admitted for investigation and control of facial pain. It was like trigeminal neuralgia and at first the cause was assumed to be a secondary in the base of her skull (from her breast cancer) compressing the nerve. The tumour responded to radiotherapy but the pain did not. Neither nerve block nor section was effective for any length of time, and I was asked if I could help.

I listened to the history of the development of her illness and she told me that when the diagnosis of breast cancer was made, she thought it was 'a huge joke'. I commented that this was an unusual way to feel about it; most people would have been upset and sad. She said that was 'not her way' and later told me why.

When she was about 8 years old, her little sister, who was very pretty and her parents' favourite child, died. Her mother was distraught with grief and the little girl tried to comfort her by saying 'But mummy, you have still got me.' 'It's not you I want,' the grieving woman blurted out, and little Lizzy retreated hastily. For months she brooded over what had been said, but her parents were too preoccupied with their sorrow to notice the suffering of their other daughter. One day her childhood exuberance returned and something she did made everyone laugh. 'At least I can cheer them up,' she thought, and she learned that if she 'clowned about' as she put it, she became popular and appreciated, which partly compensated for her deep feeling of rejection. She therefore took on this role of family clown. Her wit and intelligence enhanced it and she continued it through the ups and downs of marriage and family life. No one seemed to perceive that beneath it she was sometimes quite depressed.

When the breast cancer came, she reacted in her usual way. She was partly aware that she needed to cry and that she wanted comfort, but she did not know how to express these feelings and no one guessed their presence under the joking façade. When she developed pain, her family did understand. They showed a concern which she had not experienced before, and which she appreciated. She came to recognise that she would not lose her pain until she learned to express her real feelings and to accept emotional comfort from us, and above all from her husband. She thought he was uncaring because he did not offer her consolation; but that would be an unfamiliar role for him too. I worked with her alone and also with them as a couple. They achieved a new and more intimate understanding. Her pain never disappeared completely, but it receded into the background, enabling her to return home and live surprisingly well for six months or more. She was one of the people who felt 'almost glad' that she had had the illness, because it had brought her so many gains in self-understanding and relationship.

Other physical symptoms

Peter, whose pain was so difficult to treat while his family problems remained unsolved, also had inexplicable *nausea and vomiting*. It did not seem to be caused by his analgesics, a gastrointestinal condition, electrolyte imbalance, or any other of the common reasons for vomiting, and it was at first unresponsive to the usual anti-emetics. We came to the conclusion that he was 'worried sick' and that a cycle had developed in which he became more anxious at each meal, nauseated after a few mouthfuls, and waiting for vomiting to begin. Explanation that his vomiting was due to anxiety and not a sign that his cancer had spread or that he was more ill was an important part of management. He had been thinking that if he 'couldn't keep a thing down', he would very soon die. Although diazepam is usually the drug of choice in anxiety, a tranquilliser which is also an anti-emetic is often better in a case like his, and we chose haloperidol. He was put on fluids only, and his diet increased slowly as he gained confidence, until he was back to his usual favourites of chips and beans.

Other symptoms, especially diarrhoea, frequency of micturition, palpitations and breathlessness, can provoke a similar cycle. They are typical features of anxiety and if the patient interprets them as evidence of progress of his illness, he becomes more anxious, and, in the case of palpitations and breathlessness in particular, panic attacks may occur. All the usual medical measures must be taken to minimise the symptoms of the underlying disease. As in pain related to anxiety, the help of a relaxation therapist is beneficial. If the patient can accept that his symptoms are at least partly due to anxiety, and he is willing to learn to be aware of his breathing pattern when he begins to be anxious, he is then on the way to gaining some control of his attacks for himself. Hypnosis, particularly when the patient learns auto-hypnosis, is said to provide another method of control. As mentioned in Chapter 6, sedatives which have a respiratory depressant effect must be used with caution where there is serious lung disease. Anxiolytics may be useful in the early stages of the disease, but breathlessness which is part of the dying process itself is best managed with diamorphine and hyoscine.

Drug management

Many patients with free-floating anxiety have already been on diazepam for years and have become dependent on it, either psychologically or physically. Although they are still very anxious in spite of it, they vigorously resent an attempt to withdraw it and it is usually unwise to do so. Increasing the dose may help; very anxious patients tolerate a total of 40–60 mg a day divided into 8-hourly doses, without becoming unduly drowsy. The dose should therefore be cautiously increased from an initial 2–5 mg given at night (for the patient who has not had the drug before), until the symptoms are relieved or an unacceptable level of drowsiness is reached. Diazepam has a long half-life and therefore accumulates and may take several days to wash out after a high dose has been reduced or stopped, and due allowance must be made for this. Occasionally the patient's efforts to fight off the drowsiness result in a distressing state of sleepy agitation; quite the contrary to the desired effect. Clobazam, which is less sedating, should be tried when this happens, using a once- or twice-daily dose totalling 10–60 mg. Lorazepam is less cumulative and therefore less likely to produce excessive drowsiness. Orally it is given in a dose of 1–4 mg, rising to 10 mg if necessary and divided 6-hourly. It is useful in panic attacks, where it can be given by slow intramuscular or intravenous injection of 1–2 mg, and it carries less risk of respiratory depression or thrombophlebitis than does diazepam. If the latter is used intravenously, it should be given at a rate of not more than 5 mg per minute up to 10 mg, and it may be repeated after four hours.

When anxiety accompanies nausea and vomiting, an antiemetic tranquilliser may be a better choice than diazepam. Haloperidol in doses of 1.5–5 mg orally or by injection one to three times a day is best if the patient dislikes being drowsy. Chlorpromazine is the drug of choice if a sedative effect is desirable, and it should be given in doses of 25–100 mg 8-hourly. Haloperidol and chlorpromazine are also worth trying in anxious patients who have not responded to a benzodiazepine, and in any whose agitation has a paranoid or delusional quality. The use of these two drugs will be further discussed in the chapter on confusional states (Chapter 14).

13

Depression

It is too often assumed that depression in terminal illness is unlikely to improve. Certainly it can be difficult to treat, and some cases do not respond. Research on depressed patients admitted to a psychiatric hospital showed that those whose depression persisted for more than a year had a much higher incidence of concomitant physical illness, and a very long past history of depression. Depressed dying patients often fall into both these categories, but it is still worth attempting thorough treatment. The case history that follows is an account of the management of just such a patient, and shows how much his depression had also affected his wife and spoiled their relationship.

Mr Gray had a spinal tumour. He was 67 and his wife 63 when I first met them. Two years before, he had retired from his job as an engineer, which he enjoyed although he had never achieved as much as he thought he could. He was clever with his hands but very particular and rather slow, which often irritated his wife. She was a lively and energetic woman, probably more intelligent than her husband. She taught music at the village school nearby, and also gave piano lessons at home.

Their GP arranged for Mr Gray to come into the unit mainly because he was depressed, and the doctor felt that Mrs Gray had almost reached the end of her tether as tension increased between them. Mr Gray thought he had only come in to give his wife a rest, and he was surprised to hear that we wanted to see if we could help him.

He certainly needed help; indeed they both did. He had consulted his doctor a number of times about a pain in his back which he attributed to sitting down awkwardly on a tree trunk. When I saw him he was still very angry that nothing much was done about it until one day his legs gave way. He was admitted to hospital and a tumour was found compressing his spinal cord. His wife said the surgeon told them both the diagnosis and used the word cancer, but her husband did not take this information in, either through deafness or unwillingness to hear. An operation was performed, but it brought no relief, so he was taught to adapt to a wheelchair, which he did remarkably well for a man of his age.

Mr Gray had been depressed intermittently for many years and had been treated for it in hospital twice. Now that he was almost immobilised and could not do his usual work in his garden or even in his workshop, his depression got worse. A very independent man, he hated to be helped by his wife. He insisted on everything being done his way – and in doing everything for himself that he possibly could. She had always been very quick and efficient; it galled him to see her do things so easily. Sometimes she lost patience too, for it would so often have been quicker for her to do things for him than to let him fumble away on his own. He got grumpy and awkward. If she suggested he did something he usually enjoyed, he would refuse, depriving himself of pleasure in order to annoy her. Tension between them rose. She got a very severe and prolonged migraine (a rare thing for her) and their GP felt something just had to be done. He had expected this turn of events, for he knew Mr Gray well, having seen him for many sessions to try to help him with his depression. Earlier that year the doctor had written to the hospital: 'I cannot imagine a fate more terrible for Mr Gray than to be obliged to return to his home in a paralysed state.' The couple had just about coped before, when they could live their lives partly independently. Locked together in the necessity of giving and receiving constant and intimate care, the stress was too much.

Mr Gray, whom I soon came to call Peter, was a man who retained an air of distinguished dignity as he sat in his wheelchair with a colourful blanket over his knees. This made his frequent breaking down into quiet weeping all the more poignant. He told me at length about his misery; how he hated to be looked after, how lost he was with nothing manly he could do (he called all the occupational therapists' offerings rubbish!), how dreadfully upset he had been when he realised his wife Doreen was so ill with migraine. He had tried to reach her, fallen from his chair; tried to crawl and failed to get to her even that way.

When he wasn't being depressed, he was angry, saying the doctors treated him as if he was stupid. He also called himself stupid, saying the illness was all his own fault. He seemed convinced that it was his clumsiness in falling that brought it all on and he was full of self-blame. I thought it might help him to know that he was mistaken in his view, and so I told him that none of the doctors thought his illness was due to his fall. 'What did cause it then?' 'A disease in your bones', I replied. He seemed glad to hear that. Then his face turned grave again and he asked point blank 'Is it cancer?'. 'It is like cancer,' I replied – for it was an odd tumour, difficult to explain. 'Will it creep up until my arms are gone and I have only my head?' I told him that was *most* unlikely. 'How long have I got – 12 months?' I told him I did not know, but that I was hopeful that he had quite a long time.

He seemed less sad at the end of that interview than at the beginning, despite the news I had given him. But soon he became agitated and distressed, repeating that he had been told he had only six months to live and saying that he felt absolutely hopeless. However, when I saw him a few days later, he said he was very glad he and his wife had talked about it, although he was angry that she had known and not told him. Soon I saw her and she expressed great relief that at last he knew what the matter was. Day after day at home he had been expecting his legs to recover. Over and over again he asked her to help him to move them, or said to her 'Look, I can move my foot a bit now' when he could not. Then he would get angry that he was not progressing, blame himself, and ask why. At those times she was tempted to tell him, but restrained herself because of doubt raised by his sister. She had once said, 'If I had something like that, I wouldn't want to know,' and Doreen was not sure whether Peter really wanted to know either. So she waited and endured his querulous frustration. As soon as he knew his diagnosis the disappointed hoping and self-blame stopped. But they were replaced by fear that the growth would spread, and a preoccupation with thoughts of death. 'The real problem is,' he said, 'that I don't want to die yet.' I assured him he would not, and that we wanted to work with him to make the rest of his life as good as it could possibly be.

Knowing and sharing the diagnosis removed one cause of tension between the couple, but clearly there were others, and I focused on trying to understand why these two, who had been married 36 years and brought up two sons, should be having such difficulties. As I talked to them separately, a picture emerged of two people who were naturally 'loners'. Loyal to each other, they said little to indicate the hard times they must have had together. Doreen said only, 'We are different people in every way; but you stay together when there are children.' Peter spoke of her as 'a splendid woman who had an unhappy childhood', and he commented that if he had any complaint, it would be because of that. Doreen told how he had been depressed most of the time for about 18 years. He had that kind of obsessional depression which made him make the same miserable remarks over and over again. 'Every morning he laments that he has to face another day. The only way you can survive living with someone like that is to cut yourself off from them a bit.' Perhaps she was right, but he saw her as rather hard and uncaring sometimes. And when he refused to carry the dustbin out for her she thought it was just another bit of his awkward behaviour. Later she blamed herself sadly for that, for it was part of the beginning of his illness. Yet how was she to know? (Probably his GP was slow to examine him for similar reasons. Aches and pains are part of some people's depression and he had listened patiently to such complaints for years – and then missed the fact that this one was just a bit different.)

Peter's illness forced them to make decisions about such things as adapting the house for a wheelchair, and they had always set about decision making in totally different ways. Peter considered all the possibilities and mulled them over; with obsessional thoroughness, he worked out the consequences of each course of action. He 'slept on it', and delayed until Doreen felt nothing would ever get done. He had always been a bit like this, perhaps afraid to come to a decision in case it was a wrong one, and his illness accentuated this trait. She took stock of a situation intuitively and knew almost instantly what she wanted to do. Sometimes she just felt she could not wait, and got on with something without consulting him. Always independent, he saw this as undermining what little control he had left over his life. Now he could *do* so little, at least he wanted to be able to decide what should be done. I saw them together and we talked about how difficult it was for them both. They understood and agreed to try to meet each other half way. But events showed how hard it is to change the habits of a lifetime.

Doreen felt it would be right for her to give up teaching in order to care for Peter. He was against that as he knew she valued her independence, and he probably wanted to feel he was still well enough to be left alone for several hours at a time. Since he occasionally fell from his chair, Doreen's doubts about this made sense. A few days after our joint talk, she told me she had discussed matters with her headmaster and had given up school for the next term. In view of our recent session together, I assumed that this had been a joint decision and mentioned it to Peter, in passing. But I was wrong. Doreen had made up her mind but could not face the protracted negotiations with Peter, so she went ahead, and when I spoke to him he did not know what had been done. Naturally he was resentful, and took several days to get over this. Events proved Doreen to be right. She could cope better with his slowness and fussy ways when she did not have to hurry him to get up into his chair before she went off in the morning. Being together without many breaks did put great strain on her, but she managed it, and felt well satisfied after his death that she had done everything she could.

She was able to manage it because of her own strength and patience, and also because his depression got very much better. This was the other focus of my work. He was already on an anti-depressant, which I increased slightly. Probably more important was the fact that I 'struck a cord' with him, as he put it 'which is surprising because I have always been a loner'. He had kept himself to himself partly because of natural reserve, but partly because of the depressive belief that no one really valued him or was interested in him. He had begun to open up under the friendly influence of the district nurses who called daily. 'They are so kind,' he said 'and I don't understand why.' I guessed they perceived the lonely, rather lovable man under the grumpy exterior; and they could bear more easily with his irritating ways for they saw him for short times only – not like Doreen who had to cope much more consistently. They cared so much that when they heard he had been told his diagnosis, one travelled the 30 miles from his home village to see him. He was very touched by that.

Peter used his sessions with me to help him come to terms with his situation. He wept a lot at first, and this alternated with expressions of anger, guilt, and failure. He told me about his past – his unfulfilled ambitions, his concerns about his sons, one of whom he perceived as being just like himself. He worried about his wife and all the things which he regarded as his jobs which now fell to her. This was another area of strife – he would not let her call in outside help for repairs, for he thought no one would do the work to his satisfaction. In desperation she went up a ladder herself when the roof of their little barn leaked – and of course he was angry and fearful that she might have fallen.

Everyone caring for Peter treated him with affectionate respect, and very slowly he began to perceive that he was actually wanted and loved. After he knew his diagnosis he said about the preceding months: 'Now I understand why people started to be so nice to me; I couldn't make it out at the time.' But it was not only because he was dying that people responded thus. He had a wry humour which it was rewarding to evoke, and basically he was a very nice man. I think everyone wanted to bring out the best in him, not only for his sake, but for Doreen's, who had got so used to living with this miserable depressive that she was quite surprised to find that he could respond to fresh people in a new and more amiable way.

Later, summing up his conversations with me, Peter said: 'You have given me a new perspective. Now I want to get home and sort myself out.' He found the unit very depressing; it seemed to him like a place of death. 'I would rather die in a field than in a morgue,' was the way he put it one day. We planned for his discharge home. Doreen was worried about how he would cope, but was willing to take a chance because she knew he was a sensitive man who needed to be in his own home with familiar surroundings and not exposed to the deaths of others. Two people in his ward did die a few days before he went. He became very agitated, with nightmares, and lost his usual accurate awareness of where he was and the time of day. Perhaps we got him out just in time.

When I visited him at home ten days later, his wife reported that after initial difficulties with settling in, they were managing surprisingly well. He was still obsessed with trying to understand the frightening psychological experiences of the last few days. Probably he feared that they meant he might be going mad. He was still depressed, though not as tearful as before, and he could respond with humorous banter when I gently bullied him about his repetitive talk which got Doreen down so badly. When she was out of the room to make some tea he suddenly turned and said to me, 'Dr Stedeford, don't you honestly think I would be better off in my pram?' We talked about what this meant. It was his way of telling me how painful it was to have the knowledge and aspirations of a man combined with the helplessness of a child. I think, too, that he envied the freedom a little child has to express rage when thwarted. He was very angry about his fate and could find no way of relieving his feelings without antagonising his wife.

I never saw Peter again. But the story does not end there. As well as the district nurses, the home-care sister from our unit called weekly and she gave me progress reports. Peter's depression went on improving. I telephoned to see if he would like another visit. Doreen said that he had settled into a routine much better than she expected. He was about to get an electric wheelchair which would make him much more independent. I spoke to him as well and he was pleased with the idea of the chair. But he was still worried lest his cancer was 'sprouting out all over'. I asked if I should come again since our talks had seemed to help him before. Firmly he said he did not want 'a course of your sort of treatment', and he 'begged to be excused', but he added that I would be most welcome to come for a cup of tea if ever I was passing!

Soon the new wheelchair came and brought with it independence and further lifting of the previously most tenacious depression. The home-care sister reported that he was like a new man. The technical aspects of the chair intrigued his engineer's mind, and the freedom it gave him enabled him to go out alone again, down the village street and into the little shop. He was enjoying life more than he had for years, but it was to last only a few weeks. The cancer continued to spread. He tired easily, got up later, and did less and less. No more than the last week of his life was spent entirely in bed, cared for by his wife and the district nurses of whom he had become so fond.

I visited Doreen about two months later. She was high up a ladder, lopping a holly tree that had been darkening the house. No wonder Peter had worried about her! She was grieved, of course, but so grateful for all the help she had from friends. Above all, she was glad the depression had lifted: 'The cancer and dying were easier to bear than that' she said. What had brought it about after so many years? She thought it was the change in drugs which I had made: an increase in amitriptyline to 150 mg from the 100 mg he had received intermittently for years. In addition, facing death had changed his perspective. He began to recognise that people did care about him, and he responded. Doreen saw the changes in him and lost some of her own hopelessness. The new wheelchair certainly contributed. He was determined not to return to the unit, and the quality of care offered by his own doctor and nurses enabled him to remain at home and die peacefully there.

His story illustrates that death is not the worst that can befall a man, and that persistent care by a team of people who know how to help can overcome even very long-standing problems. Doreen wished they had received such help much sooner, but perhaps it took a jolt of knowing life was to be short to shake him loose from his entrenched depressive routine sufficiently for this change to take place.

Diagnosis of depression

Distinguishing between sadness and depressive illness requiring active treatment is difficult in the terminally ill. The biological indicators such as disturbed sleep, constipation, loss of appetite, weight, and libido, can all be direct effects of the illness, as can weakness, weariness, and emotional liability with a tendency to cry more readily than usual. However, the depressive pattern of early morning waking may emerge more clearly when pain has been controlled and a night sedative has helped the patient to get off to sleep satisfactorily. To make a diagnosis, more reliance than usual must be placed on the content of what the patient says – looking particularly for indications of *low self-esteem* and *undue guilt*. The newly admitted patient may say that he is a burden to his family and it would be better if he were dead. This may be depressive, or it may be a response to a real situation in which his family have become exhausted and he has helplessly watched them become worn out. If it is the latter, he will cease to feel a burden once he knows he is welcome in the hospital, and he sees his family recovering from their fatigue. Depressive ideas are not so easily lost, and an interview with the relatives may confirm that their view is not at all like that of the patient. Mrs N. (Chapter 9) devalued herself in this way, saying that it would be better if she died quickly and got out of the way so that her husband could marry again while he was still young. In fact he was very fond of her and had no such ideas in mind. When she had been on amitriptyline for two weeks she stopped talking like this, recognising that she was precious to her husband and that he wanted her to live for as long as possible.

Similarly, a depressed patient may feel an exaggerated sense of guilt for things that have happened in the past. Such a man told me that he had been reviewing his life and that he had come to the conclusion that he should never have married; that doing so had ruined his wife's life completely, and that she would have been a much happier woman without him. When I saw her she agreed that there had been quite serious problems from time to time between them, but that she had contributed equally to them. She recognised that he had lost sight of all the good memories which in her mind compensated for the bad.

In terminal illness, *suicidal ideas* are not necessarily an indication of severe depression. They may reflect an understandable wish not to be a burden, or they may be the result of a mistaken assumption that nothing can be done to relieve intolerable pain. As soon as the social situation improves or the pain is brought under control, such patients are in less of a hurry to die. A woman like this asked for euthanasia, saying that 'you would not let a dog suffer as I have recently'. I told her I understood her request very well in view of what I knew about her suffering over the past few weeks, but I asked her if she would be willing to wait a few days to see if we could improve things before we talked further about it. Four days later I returned for our promised interview, and found her sitting out of bed, cheerful and eagerly looking forward to a visitor. I did not raise the topic again as it would have been incongruous in the changed situation.

A few patients who talk about suicide are expressing their wish to be as fully in control of their lives as possible. They are angry that this most important event is likely to happen at an unknown time and in an unknown way. Defiantly, they would rather choose the moment and mode of their death than leave it to chance. For a very few patients, the appraisal that the situation is bleak and hopeless is realistic, evoking our sympathy and understanding. Anti-depressants will not help when this is the case, and the patient should be made as comfortable as possible, using sedatives where necessary to relieve emotional distress, bearing in mind that the relief of this kind of suffering in the dying is as important as the relief of pain.

Truly depressive suicidal ideas are usually related to feelings of unworthiness and guilt, with a sense that the patient deserves to die. They may have a more obvious delusional quality, the patient believing, for example, that his cancer is contagious and that he should kill himself to spare his family. Indeed the stress of the physical illness and the knowledge of impending death may precipitate manic or depressive illness, especially in patients who have a personal and/or family history of this. It should also be remembered that both terminal illness and depression are so common that they will occasionally occur together without the one being the cause of the other.

Anti-depressants

For those depressed patients with a terminal illness who are not on medication that interacts with anti-depressants, the drug management is the same as in other depressives. Frail patients, like elderly ones, are more prone to confusion when on anti-depressants, and therefore their treatment should begin with small doses and be cautiously increased. Even in quite ill patients, larger doses may be tolerated well and be essential to procure a response. Doses should therefore be increased gradually until there is improvement, or side-effects are persistently intolerable, and the highest acceptable dose should be maintained for at least two or three weeks before it is assumed to be ineffective.

The tricyclic drugs are the first choice, unless the patient in question is already experiencing marked anti-cholinergic side-effects from other medications, especially dry mouth and constipation. For the anxious depressed patient, amitriptyline is best, given in one dose at night, starting with 25–75 mg and working up to 150 mg (or rarely even up to 300 mg). Dothiepin is better tolerated by some patients and its actions are similar. The retarded patient does better on imipramine, which is less sedating and is used in the same dose range as amitriptyline.

When it is important to minimise anti-cholinergic and cardiovascular side-effects, or a change of anti-depressant has to be tried because these have become intolerable, one of the newer drugs should be used. Mianserin is sedative and is given in a single night-time dose starting with 30–90 mg and increasing if necessary right up to 200 mg. Nomiphensine is not sedative and can be given in a single morning dose, or in divided doses totalling 75–200 mg per day.

When a response has been obtained, the dose level should be maintained for at least a month, and then it may be gradually reduced to a maintenance dose of about half the initial one, provided symptoms do not return. When the prognosis is short, it is better not to risk relapse by further dose reduction unless the patient becomes more ill and side-effects become a serious problem.

Electroconvulsive therapy

The idea of giving electroconvulsive therapy (ECT) to a person who is very ill and may only live another few weeks is not often considered by many doctors. Yet severe depression can cause more suffering than physical illness, and these are the patients who cannot afford to wait two or three weeks for anti-depressants to take effect. The following case history illustrates the use of ECT in such a patient.

Mr Williamson, aged 58, had widespread abdominal cancer (primary unknown) and he was very ill with an enlarged liver and intermittent subacute intestinal obstruction when first admitted to our care. Much more distressing to him and his family was his severe depression. He had already been depressed for some months, with only partial response to treatment, and as he got worse he presented a pitiful picture of obsessional rumination and agitation. A year previously one of his children had died in appalling circumstances, and in his depression he became convinced that he was partly responsible for the tragedy. Through every waking moment he was going over what he might have done to prevent it, and reproaching himself in his morbid guilt. Sustained conversation was not possible, and he was only quiet (but not peaceful) if he was heavily sedated. From his wife I learned that he was normally a quiet, thoughtful man who would have been using this time to prepare himself and his family for his death. Such activity had been eclipsed by his psychiatric illness and the family were grieved not only by his suffering but also by the fact that he was being denied the dignified death of which they knew he was capable.

Recognising that we had very little time, I approached colleagues and his wife suggesting that we use ECT. Some staff were at first sceptical, but as they saw how miserably we were failing to control his distress, they agreed that it should be tried. His wife accepted the idea readily because the patient's brother had suffered from similar depression and his response to ECT had been remarkable. Obtaining his agreement was a problem. It was not possible if he was heavily sedated, and when he was awake he could not be diverted from his ruminations for long enough to attend to anything. In the circumstances, no one wanted to use the powers of the Mental Health Act to treat him without his consent. His wife did her utmost to get through to him to explain what was planned, and persuade him that it was for the best. He seemed to understand her. We let him lighten from his sedation and used the brief interval before agitation took over completely to obtain his formal consent.

The treatments were given on alternate days. After the first one he was calm and rational for only two hours; then we had to revert to our previous regime of sedation. After the second the improvement lasted almost a day and he then relapsed, but after the third he became 'his normal self' according to his wife, and remained so until his death a week later. During that time he had a birthday. Propped up in bed, he read his cards and could enjoy brief visits. He took in the news that his son had obtained a very good job, and he talked affectionately and sadly to his wife about his dying. Any who had misgivings about ECT beforehand lost them as they saw the change it had brought about in this man.

When giving ECT to such an ill patient, it is important to consult with the anaesthetist well beforehand so that he can adjust his premedication and management, if necessary, to take into account the drugs already being used, especially if these include steroids, as they did in this case. The risk of fracture at the site of a secondary deposit in bone should be borne in mind. Provided an adequate dose of muscle relaxant is used to produce a well-modified fit, this risk is probably less than that incurred in moving and turning the patient in the course of regular care. If possible, it is better for the ECT team from the nearest psychiatric hospital to come to the patient, rather than transporting him to them. If nursing problems are not too great, he can be temporarily transferred if liaison between the two hospitals is good. Continuity of care can be assured and anxieties lessened if medical and nursing staff accustomed to the care of dying patients can visit him there.

However thorough the care, a few patients will die in the state that Mr Williamson was before effective treatment. The lesson to be learned from the cases in this chapter is that some can recover, and therefore it is worthwhile for their sake and their family's to use all available resources in a well-planned effort to obtain maximum relief.

14

Confusion

People who are very ill, and especially those who are near to death, often suffer from a variety of disturbing experiences, commonly referred to as confusion. When this happens, no one should assume that it is an inevitable concomitant of the illness for which little can be done other than provide sedation. Many of the conditions are treatable, and even when they are not, much of the distress they cause to patients, relatives, and others in close contact with them can often be relieved.

The term 'confused' is often used loosely to refer to a wide range of symptoms including disorientation in time and place, inappropriate behaviour of all kinds, memory failure, hallucinations, talking nonsense, and paranoia. The causative agent can be equally varied: drug effects, biochemical and metabolic disturbances, primary and secondary brain tumours, or the psychological stress related to dying. Effective treatment depends on accurate diagnosis both in terms of the phenomena the patient is experiencing and their likely cause. Equally essential is a willingness to try to understand these patients. They have lost touch with reality as we know it, and are often very frightened, particularly as they are usually at least partly aware that something extraordinary is happening to them and they suspect that they may be going mad. Other people find them disturbing because they do not know how to talk to them or what to do to help them. Too often the emphasis in treatment is on control because their behaviour is disruptive and upsets other patients. If their suffering is to be relieved, a more refined approach combining knowledge with sensitivity is needed.

Understanding many of the experiences of confused patients is made easier if a model first used in the study of schizophrenia is employed. This model postulates that there is a filter which controls the entry of stimuli into awareness, from the environment, the body, and the unconscious. This is represented by the

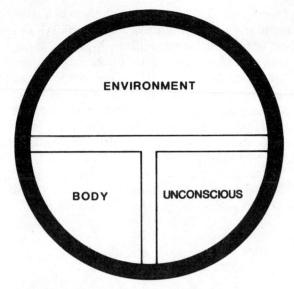

Fig. 14.1 The filter circumscribing awareness.

circumference of the circle in Fig. 14.1. The area of awareness within the circle is partitioned to indicate that people normally know from which of the three sources information is coming at any one time. Awareness of, for example, every sound, the touch of clothes, the heart beat, and all the contents of the memory store, would be totally overwhelming and it is essential for normal functioning that most of this is excluded. The filter permits selection and allows the intensity of the experience to be varied, in the same way that a radio has both tuning and volume control.

Table 14.1 Factors influencing permeability of the filter

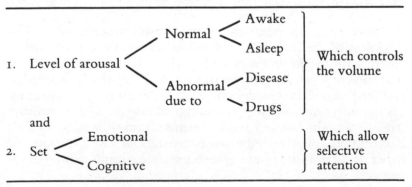

It can be seen from Table 14.1 that the level of arousal is like volume control and that 'set' allows for selectivity. This concept of set is best explained by examples. A person who has been sitting by the fireside listening to ghost stories has a fearful emotional set. Then the creak of the stairs or the flap of a curtain in a night breeze may be startling, whereas in other circumstances it would pass almost unnoticed. A mother who knows that her baby is ill and might vomit in the night (her cognitive set) will sleep soundly through loud traffic but would wake at the baby's slightest stirring.

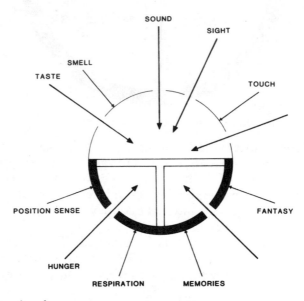

Fig. 14.2 Awake.

Figure 14.2 represents a normal person when awake. The thickness of the filter is varied to indicate that most experience enters from the environment. Only those bodily sensations that require action, such as hunger or a full bladder, reach awareness, and the person has considerable control over what he is thinking about and remembering, although thoughts and memories irrelevant to the task in hand do intrude from time to time. This control is usually referred to as concentration. The partitions are intact, indicating that he is able to separate stimuli from various sources.

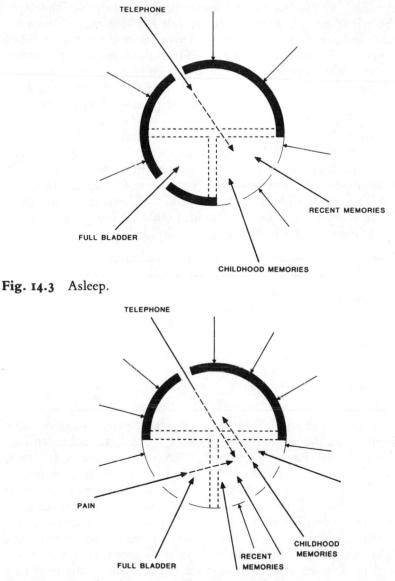

Fig. 14.3 Asleep.

Fig. 14.4 Confused.

Figure 14.3 represents the normal person when asleep. Most experience comes from the unconscious in the form of dreams, and almost all stimuli from the environment and the body are excluded. Only those that require urgent action get through. The partitions are incomplete. A full bladder may provoke a disturbed dream before the person awakes, and anyone who has been on call knows how the ring of the telephone may be woven into the moments of a dream just before waking.

Figure 14.4 represents confusion. Impairment of consciousness for whatever cause decreases the permeability of the filter for environmental stimuli. Awareness of the body seems to be increased or distorted and material that usually remains unconscious appears as vivid memories or hallucinations. The partitions break down and the patient may be wrong in his perception of the source of his experience. It is understandable that he may be distressed or terrified and behave accordingly. Those around him who have no idea what his inner world is like at that moment are baffled and may feel helpless.

Table 14.2 Components of disturbed experiences

Patient	Level of arousal	Stimulus	Set	Experience
1	Deeply asleep	+ High temperature	+ Afraid of death	→ Nightmare of burning to death
2	Drugged	+ Stranger	+ Guilty	→ Misperception of stranger as a policeman; attempts to escape
3	Drowsy	+ Stranger	+ Longing to see mother	→ Misperception of stranger as mother

Table 14.2 shows how three common experiences may come about when the influences of level of arousal, stimulus, and set are combined. Patient number 1, who is deeply asleep, feverish, and afraid that he may soon die, may have a nightmare that he is burning to death. From the table, the components of treatment are obvious: waking him up as fully as possible and treating his fever may be sufficient to calm him down. But it is not always so, and in this situation he may respond to a gentle invitation to talk about anything that is frightening him. Where fear is suppressed or denied, it may sometimes find expression in this way as a recurrent nightmare. It is preferable to explore such fears with the patient there and then if he is willing. Next morning he may have 'forgotten' it or be reluctant to talk about it further. Nightmares like this often stop when the underlying fear has been openly recognised.

Dying patients often review their lives and feel guilty about aspects of their past. If their consciousness is impaired, they may mistakenly think a stranger is someone who has come to arrest or punish them, and they may attempt to escape (patient number 2). Some of them will be helped by a priest or psychotherapist in whom they can confide, who will help them to accept what has happened and perhaps to attempt a reconciliation or to make amends. Dying patients also go over good memories. They are often living in the past and expecting to see relatives to whom they have been close. If they are drowsy, they may think, for instance, that a nurse who approaches the bedside is their mother (patient number 3). The nurse then has to decide how she will respond. If she does not correct the misperception and the patient then becomes lucid, he may realise his mistake and feel angry that he is being humoured. A better alternative is to say gently, 'No, I am not your mother, but I guess you wish that I was,' and then to talk to and care for the patient in the motherly way that he is needing.

The distinction between a misperception, of which the last two cases are examples, and an hallucination, is important as the management is different.

> Mrs K. complained to the night staff that she could hear people talking about her and laughing at her. She thought such things should not be allowed to happen in hospital and she wanted to discharge herself. The nurses reported that she was hallucinating. When the sister sat quietly with her for a time, she also heard laughter and voices. They were coming from the nearby kitchen. The patient could only partly hear what was being said, and like most very ill people, she was preoccupied with herself and assumed that the conversations referred to her. She improved when she was moved to a quieter room and her sedation reduced. If she had been treated for her 'hallucinations' with chlorpromazine, she might have been made worse.

Mrs K. was misperceiving something that was really there. Hallucinations are sensory experiences without external stimuli. A visual or auditory memory that would normally be unconscious is released into awareness; or a sensory area of the brain is stimulated, for example by a tumour, producing phenomena like those of temporal lobe epilepsy. Treatment should be aimed at suppression of the abnormal experience, either with haloperidol or a phenothiazine, or, in the case of a tumour, an anti-convulsant may be more appropriate. Patients in any of these groups may have become so ill that a sustained conversation is impossible; nor do they respond to the reassuring touch or presence of a familiar person. Then medication must be used to relieve their distress. It will be clear that if one cause of the problem is impairment of consciousness, a small dose of a sedative may make the situation worse. Even a large one may silence the screams of the nightmare or make the patient too inco-ordinated to run away, without relieving the mental turmoil. The choice and use of drugs for these patients will be discussed later in the chapter.

Table 14.3   Common causes of confusion

Medication	Most drugs acting on the CNS
	Steroids
Infection	Whether pyrexial or not
Trauma	Head injury
	Subdural haematoma
Tumour	Cerebral primary or secondaries
	Malignant disease elsewhere
Cerebrovascular disease	Strokes
	Dementia
Cardiac and respiratory failure	Anoxia
	Hypercapnia
Biochemical and metabolic	Electrolyte imbalance
	dehydration
	hyponatraemia
	hypokalaemia
	Hypercalcaemia
	Uraemia
	Hepatic failure
	Hypoglycaemia
General discomfort	Full bladder or bowel
	Uncomfortable bedding
	Pruritus

When a patient becomes confused, the use of a check list like that in Table 14.3 should lead to the diagnosis of treatable causes. Medication is most important, and investigation should begin with a review of the drugs that the patient is receiving. One reason for excessive medication is that as symptoms worsen or new ones develop, prescribers tend to add new drugs or increase current ones without giving due consideration to cumulative effects and interactions. Night sedatives should not be used to procure sleep if a patient is being kept awake by a specific treatable cause, for example pain, anxiety, or insomnia due to depression. When drugs are given for any of these conditions, it may be appropriate to reduce or omit the current night sedative. On the other hand, sudden withdrawal of a drug that the patient has used for years, for example, diazepam, a barbiturate, or of course alcohol, may also precipitate confusion.

When the introduction of a new drug is followed by confusion, it should be withdrawn, and if necessary a drug from a slightly different class substituted to see if improvement ensues. It should not be assumed that medication that has been given for some time before the onset of the confusion cannot be the cause of it. The drug may have gradually reached toxic levels because of its long half-life (for example diazepam) or because the patient metabolises and excretes it less effectively due to the progressive nature of his illness.

The filter model can usefully provide a way of thinking about how drugs cause confusion. Sedatives can be perceived as decreasing the permeability of the filter to stimuli from the environment so that less information is taken in. (In depression and anxiety also, and in severe pain, the patient is so preoccupied with his experience that stimuli from the outside world do not register. He may then appear disorientated, not knowing the time of day or where he is, and testing him may also reveal impairment of short-term memory. This syndrome should not be mistaken for early dementia, which it resembles. It is reversible if the underlying cause can be treated, and the patient like this who is worried that he is dementing should be reassured.)

Stimulants increase the permeability of the filter so that signals are perceived as more intense and the patient over-reacts. Drugs that produce hallucinations, nightmares, paranoia and other psychotic states may act by increasing the permeability of the filter to unconscious material. The psychoses occasionally caused by steroids can be viewed in this way too. The whole picture of the acute brain syndrome or delirium can be viewed as a release phenomenon. There is a slackening of the control the patient usually maintains over the expression of his personality.

The naturally timid person may become terrified, the slightly suspicious becomes paranoid, the anxious becomes agitated, and the depressed becomes suicidal. Unpleasant memories which have been suppressed, and the more primitive parts of the unconscious which are usually inaccessible in health, may enter awareness.

A full discussion of drug effects and interactions likely to precipitate confusion would not be appropriate here; Davison's paper[1] on toxic psychosis provides excellent lists and descriptions. In dying patients particular attention should be paid to idiosyncratic responses to analgesics. About 10% of patients experience hallucinosis or nightmares in response to narcotic analgesics, and pentazocine is the worst offender. Tricyclic anti-depressants may cause agitation, especially in the elderly, and some beta-blockers (especially propranolol) produce vivid dreams and hallucinations. Other drugs commonly implicated in one or other of the phenomena of confusion are anti-Parkinsonian drugs (especially benzhexol), anti-convulsants (especially phenytoin), anti-inflammatory drugs (especially indomethacin), and drugs used to control hyperacidity (especially cimetidine).

Most other items in Table 14.3 are self-explanatory. Investigations should only be carried out if the results obtained are likely to be helpful in management. Patients and relatives are sometimes relieved to know that the cause of the problem is a brain tumour. For them this does not seem to carry a stigma in the same way that inexplicable insanity does. How actively a condition like hypercalcaemia should be treated depends on the extent of the underlying condition, usually malignant disease with bony secondaries. If the patient has other problems that have made life scarcely worth living for him, the hypercalcaemia can be regarded as a terminal event and its effects treated symptomatically; but if the patient has been reasonably well, active treatment should be attempted. We have had more than one patient admitted with a diagnosis of terminal confusion who has returned home after treatment and lived well for several weeks or months.

> The case of Mrs N. illustrates why 'general discomfort' has been included. She was a very alert old lady who told the night staff that 'something awful is going on, and I must get out of here

immediately.' It was difficult to restrain her from leaving there and then in her night-clothes. Eventually one of the nurses noticed that she had a full bladder and catheterising her restored her mental state to normal. As the model explains, in her drowsy state she was unable to know whether the source of her acute discomfort came from her body or from outside, and she thought she might best escape from it by running away.

Failure to recognise that the illness is the cause of a worsening condition is a common reason for very ill patients wishing to discharge themselves. They remember that they were less ill when they were at home, and they assume therefore that something being done to them in hospital (usually the medication they are receiving) is what is making them worse. This is another example of the use of denial and projection to avoid the painful knowledge 'I am dying', and it leads to the development of paranoid ideas. These will be further discussed in Chapter 15.

Patients with slowly progressive brain tumours have many symptoms of confusion, and the following case history illustrates some aspects of management.

Ruby was 58, and had a parietal lobe tumour that had been present for 10 years. At first it caused fits which were well controlled, but gradually over the year before admission she became partially paralysed and her speech was impaired. She was a widow whose husband never came back from Germany after the war. When he left she had just become pregnant and she returned to live with her mother who brought up her baby son while she went to work to support them both. Now the son had left home and the mother was in her eighties, unable to care for Ruby anymore.

She was very quiet and withdrawn when she was first admitted. All day she sat with her eyes closed, looking unhappy but apparently inaccessible to anyone. The unit had been open only a few months and none of us was very experienced in caring for a patient like this, but we all felt there ought to be a way to reach her. After several fruitless attempts during which I sat with her quietly or asked questions which were met with stony silences, she answered one. I had said that I wondered what she thought about all day, especially as she looked so sad. 'The tumour growing in my head' was the blunt reply. 'What would you most like us to do for you?' I asked. 'Shrivel it up.' Very gently I said that I thought we both knew that this could not be done. 'If we tried our best to help you to find peace of mind and courage, would that also be worthwhile?' I asked. 'Yes.'

I told some of the nurses about our conversation. Encouraged by my success they also tried harder to communicate with Ruby, but usually she remained unresponsive. One day she was distressed and kept saying, 'The hospital won't be here much longer.' Several people tried to reassure her or distract her from this, but she was adamant. I was asked to help. My intuitive response taught me a lesson about talking with confused patients: if the *content* of what they say does not make sense, listen to the *mood*. 'Ruby, it sounds as if something awful is going to happen,' I said. 'Yes.' 'Might it be to you?' 'Yes.' She was using projection; thinking that the coming disaster would be outside herself, not inside, and by correcting it we were able to talk again about herself, and her distress ceased.

Ruby had a dense hemiplegia by now and fell out of her chair unless she was held there by the tray fastened in front of her. One day she angrily told her relatives, 'The nurses won't let me walk. I know I can, but they won't let me.' The family believed this and challenged the ward sister. Two nurses tried to help Ruby to walk but she could not. 'I could yesterday. I am just tired,' she said. 'You just won't let me walk.' She was using projection again. Unable to bear the knowledge that her tumour had spread so far, she felt better if she blamed her problem on us. In a sense, by tolerating her accusations, we were temporarily bearing her burden for her. I explained this to the staff and the family and they understood.

Sometimes Ruby was living in the past. She seemed to be wandering in Germany, searching for her husband, calling to him and crying. We learned how to stop this for her, at least temporarily, by taking her hands and calling her name firmly. When we had her attention we could remind her that it had all happened long ago, that she was now safely with us, and that we would do all we could to help her.

Dying patients often relive frightening incidents in their lives, especially if they have been close to death before. It is almost as if the psyche, in trying to make some sense of the present fear, asks itself 'when did I last feel like this?', and the memories that have been suppressed for so long are released as vividly as if the events were happening all over again. One patient like this kept describing a plane crash he was in, and another thought he was once again a prisoner of war in a concentration camp. At first it may be hard to understand what the patient is talking about, and relatives should be asked if they know about the events in question. These patients sometimes benefit from being able to go over the story again with someone else. Others, like Ruby, need help to separate past and present. For a few, nothing brings relief and heavy sedation is required.

One day Ruby complained to me that 'something was going on'. She was worried about who was caring for her mother, and her sister and son would not tell her anything. At her request I met them and discovered that the family was divided about who should be responsible, and that the mother was unwell and very unhappy. They had not told Ruby because 'she has enough on her plate, she does not want any more worries'. I pointed out that she felt guilty that she could not longer look after her mother. All she could offer now was her concern and advice, and it was wrong to deprive her of the opportunity to go on giving these. They saw the point and began to include her in the discussions of family affairs again, particularly when I reminded them that it was probably better for her to be worried about other people than totally preoccupied with herself.

Often Ruby was very confused and her conversation made no sense. A few inexperienced nurses talked about her in her presence, and one day she said to me 'Those nurses think I am mad.' It is always better to assume that a patient is more sane than he seems. Often those like Ruby have lucid intervals and know that their previous behaviour has been abnormal. The dread of insanity is for them greater than the fear of death. They are helped by being told 'Whatever odd things your tumour (or drugs, or illness) makes you say or do, we know that you *yourself* are all right.' They learn to separate 'myself' from 'my illness' and can sometimes even laugh at their mishaps, especially if staff are sufficiently good humoured and tolerant.

Ruby could not see clearly and wore a large watch on a ribbon around her neck. One day she was banging it angrily on her tray, complaining that it was always wrong. I looked at it and told her that today it was not. Amongst the jumble of words that followed I heard her say something about a hundred minutes. In her work the decimalisation of the pound must have made a great impression as she had been a book-keeper. I wondered out loud whether she thought they had now decimalised time, and indeed she did. Unable to accept that her own sense of time was disturbed, she had to find another cause for the problem. If it was not her watch, it must be 'them'. I assured her that they had not, and she was quiet for a while. Then she said 'It is only a matter of time.' There was no confusion now. We talked about how hard it was for her, not knowing how much time she had left, and she speculated about what would happen to her in the near future. This was a moment of great closeness and following it she became more accessible to other people too, especially the nurses. On good days she could join in their jokes, and on bad days she could accept comfort from them. I withdrew as others took over, for it was important that she should not be dependent on me alone, especially since I could usually only see her three times a week.

Ruby died peacefully a month or so later. No single patient has taught me as much as she did, and I leave the last words of her story to her. One lucid day, when we had been talking about how muddled she often was, she looked me straight in the eye and asserted, 'I think it is perfectly logical that I should be confused.'

The use of drugs

The importance of reducing or stopping any unnecessary drugs has already been emphasised. The specific syndromes of hallucinosis and paranoia are best treated with haloperidol. In the physically ill and the elderly, 1.5 mg two or three times daily may suffice. In the more robust patient, treatment should begin with 5 mg two or three times daily. Emergencies such as mania may require that haloperidol be given by intramuscular injection, 10 mg every two hours until control is achieved, changing to the oral route and reducing the dose as soon as the acute phase subsides. Parkinsonian side-effects are seldom encountered when haloperidol is used in this way, and anti-cholinergic drugs (e.g. orphenadrine) should only be added if dose reduction is ineffective, or in the rare emergency of an acute dystonic reaction. Chlorpromazine is preferable only if its sedative effect is needed to enable the patient to sleep until the mental turmoil is relieved. The slurring of speech and the drowsiness which it produces add to some patients' distress. An initial dose of 150 mg in tablet or syrup form, or 100 mg by deep intramuscular injection may be repeated six-hourly until control is achieved. Occasionally very disturbed patients need much more – up to 1 g in 24 hours. Postural hypotension is the foremost complication, and patients on high doses must be in bed, at least initially. When chlorpromazine is being used to control a very disturbing psychotic state, the dose level should be determined by the mental state (e.g. speech content, facial expression, eye movements) and not only by the level of consciousness. A long sleep after a large dose does not necessarily mean that too much was used. The patient may have been exhausted by his terrifying experiences and may need to sleep to recover. The side-effect of sedation is no more relevant in determining the right dose of anti-psychotic drugs in psychosis than it is in determining the dose of analgesic to be used for pain control.

Anxiety and agitation *not* associated with hallucinations or psychosis are best treated with diazepam, where sedation is an advantage, or clobazam where it is not. The use of these drugs is described in Chapter 12. Occasionally a patient who does not respond well to a benzodiazepine benefits more from a small dose of haloperidol. Conversely, a patient needing haloperidol may benefit from the addition of a small dose of diazepam as an anxiolytic, rather than a change-over to chlorpromazine. It is not usually necessary to use both classes of drug, but where symptom control proves difficult, the trial of a combination is justified.

Toward the very end of life, diamorphine and hyoscine together may be more effective than anything else in producing a tranquil state. The dose of diamorphine will usually be determined by the level previously required by the patient, and this can be combined with 400–800 μg of hyoscine, both drugs being repeated every four hours.

The care of dying patients who are confused requires knowledge and skill, together with a readiness to abandon a clinical attitude occasionally, in favour of an intuitive response. Sometimes a gesture, a silence, or some very simple act meets the need best. A psychodynamic explanation of what happened in the following vignette could be that I helped the patient, who was a priest, by reaffirming his accustomed role, with all that meant for him. Some readers will see in it something more.

The patient, aged 60, was in kidney failure as a result of the spread of his cancer. He was very withdrawn, his posture and expression indicating that he was suffering considerably, but he did not speak to anyone who came to his bedside to try to help him. The first time I saw him I felt completely helpless too. Sitting with him, I talked quietly to him, but did not know if he heard me or not.

The next time I came, he was slumped in a chair, looking as if he desperately needed to lie down and sleep, although he persistently refused to be helped into bed. The preceding night had been disturbed by nightmares and he had remained inaccessible to comfort. He seemed determined to stay awake if he could, rather than risk further distress. While I was wondering what to do, I noticed that a cup of tea had been left for him. I asked him if he would like some, but got no response, so I decided to try to help him to drink. I wondered if doing something together might somehow break down the barrier between us. Gently, I encouraged him to wrap his hand around the cup and we raised it to his lips. He sipped a few times, then stopped and opened his eyes. It felt strange to me that I was helping a priest to drink, and I said to him 'Over the years you must have given a cup to many people.' Our eyes met. Nothing more was said, but he began to relax. Sensing that he was ready to sleep, I asked the nurses to try again to help him into bed. This time he went willingly, and he remained peacefully there for the last two days of his life.

Reference

1. Davison K. (1981). Toxic psychosis. *British Journal of Hospital Medicine*; **26/5**:530–37. (Some of the material in this paper was first published in Stedeford A. (1978). Understanding confusional states. *British Journal of Hospital Medicine*; **20/6**.)

15

Paranoid reactions and other problems

Paranoid reactions

Paranoid reactions are quite common in very ill and dying patients. They can occur as part of a confusional state, and may be precipitated by a number of the conditions in the check list in Chapter 14 (Table 14.3), particularly the use of steroids. In these patients the paranoid ideas come and go with the fluctuation of their confusion, and are usually worse at night. As already described, treatment should be aimed at the underlying condition wherever possible. In other patients the problem occurs without other psychiatric symptoms, as a psychogenic paranoid reaction. The psychodynamic aspects of treatment are particularly important here.

Mr F. had carcinomatosis and seemed to have accepted that he was dying. He had been in the First World War and said he had got used to death then. As an old soldier, he was not afraid of it. As he became more ill, he began to believe that the people visiting the patient in the opposite bed were plotting to kill him. Soon he was so convinced of this that he attempted to hit one of them with his walking stick. He was surprisingly strong and this provoked a crisis. Nothing would shake his belief and he was rather angry when I suggested that he might really be worried because his illness was getting worse. At this stage he denied that he was seriously ill at all. He was given 5 mg of haloperidol and I returned to see him the next day. Then he was less convinced about the plot and more ready to talk. I went over the history of his illness again, helping him to acknowledge the evident deterioration in his health. I said that most people in his position – even old soldiers – would be worried and at least a little frightened that they might be going to die. He wept quietly as he admitted that he felt that way too. He was very ashamed of his tears, and I told him that it was physical weakness that made them come more easily than usual, and that we thought it perfectly natural for a man in his position to cry from time to time. This consoled him slightly. The next day the paranoid ideas had gone completely; intermittently he was sad, but they did not recur. For a time he had not been able to tolerate the knowledge that he was dying and used denial and projection, saying 'I am not dying; they are going to kill me.'

The patient who wishes to fight his illness may use this mechanism, for it is easier to think that the cause of the problem is an external one. Then the patient feels safe. What he needs to do is destroy the attacker, escape from the dangerous environment, or refuse to take the drugs that are poisoning him. Suspicion that medicine is making them worse is a common problem in the dying. In hospital most patients are observant about what their neighbours are given and notice when someone starts on a new medicine or begins to receive injections, and dies soon afterwards. Sometimes they conclude that the treatment was given to accelerate death, and they fear that they are next on the list, especially if they have been offered 'some of the same'. They may endure considerable pain rather than take it. If explanations from staff are not accepted, these patients need to be given haloperidol for their mental state, but they usually refuse to take anything new. Sometimes they will accept it from a nurse they particularly like and trust. Others will allow themselves to be persuaded by their family doctor whom they have known for years, or by a relative, and enlisting their help may be the best solution. It is never appropriate to attempt to conceal medication in food or drink for these patients. If they recognise what has been done, their belief that they are being poisoned will be re-enforced. Refusal of medication that is not absolutely essential should be respected in these circumstances. When pain gets worse or other symptoms recur, the patient may be willing to take it again and may accept the haloperidol also then. Almost always, tactful but firm persuasion works in the end.

Morbid jealousy

In two patients who had breast cancer treated by mastectomy, the rather rare syndrome of morbid jealousy developed as a circumscribed delusional system. It probably occurs more often in a milder form, under-reported because of the embarrassment and stress it causes to the family. The husbands of these two patients suffered greatly and the children were drawn in, uncertain which parent to believe.

Charles and Penny were in their forties and their marriage was a good one, but 'not perfect' they both said. When one of her breasts was replaced by a disfiguring scar, Penny found it hard to believe that her husband loved her just as much as before. Treatment with steroids made her gain weight, and chemotherapy caused her to lose her hair. She knew she was not as attractive as she used to be, and felt that her husband would inevitably look elsewhere for his sexual satisfaction.

Hanging unused in her wardrobe were some lovely clothes that no longer fitted her. When Charles's secretary complained in the office that she had nothing new to wear for her holiday, he thought it might be a good idea to give her one or two of his wife's discarded dresses, which were just her size. Penny could see that it was a sensible and generous thing to do and she agreed, but then she began to wonder. If her husband was late home or away on business, she began to suspect that he was having an affair. She started to check up on him and found 'evidence', convincing to her although not to anyone else. He could not reassure her and her accusations produced distressing rows between them. As he said to me, 'What makes it hardest is that I have been tempted and have *not* acted. I hate the fact that she does not trust me.' He had no idea that her problem might be directly connected with her illness. She began to tell friends of her suspicions and some thought she might be right. Her husband consulted his general practitioner, who did not seem able to help very much. One night, after a particularly painful row, Penny locked herself in her car and threatened suicide. The children had overheard the quarrel and their father was very concerned about the effect on them. Next time he brought his wife to see the radiotherapist he told him what had been going on, and Penny was admitted to our unit, ostensibly for some investigations, but really in order that I could see her.

I heard the story from each of them and made the diagnosis of morbid jealousy, not on the basis of the husband's denial that he was having an extra-marital affair, but on the nature of Penny's 'evidence'. To her, small things like a stain on his clothes or a sweet paper in his pocket were absolute proof that he had another woman, probably his secretary. After all, hadn't he even given her some of her own prettiest clothes!

I tried to explain to her that when a woman's appearance changes and she knows she is less attractive, and especially if she no longer wants sex very often, it is natural for her to wonder how her husband is coping. I sympathised warmly with her and made her feel that I understood what she was going through. Then I told her that sometimes being suspicious was part of an illness, like being depressed or anxious can be. She was dubious about that idea but reluctantly agreed to try the haloperidol I wanted to giver her, to see if it made any difference. She was unwilling to talk about her husband again over the next few days, but soon he reported that she was less resentful toward him and was no longer asking accusatory questions. Within two weeks she behaved almost normally with him when he visited. When I asked her about her thoughts at that stage, she said she still wondered whether he was faithful or not, but she dwelt on it less, and it did not worry her so much. She was longing to go home as she was fairly well physically and realised that she did not need to be in hospital. We agreed to a weekend visit and she was better, but not as friendly toward her husband as she had been while she was in the unit.

Within another week or two all talk of an affair ceased, and it never returned during the remaining year of her life. She had to be re-admitted several times as her illness progressed, and she said the suspicions remained 'in the background' but she could easily dismiss them. She felt insecure away from her husband and spent much of the last part of her life at home, nursed mainly by him. He became exhausted as he attempted to give her all the care she needed, while still keeping on his job. In the enforced intimacy of toiletting and dressing, the couple became very close in a new way, which brought joy as well as sadness. She died at home, with his arms around her.

Manic reactions

Hypomania, or a manic reaction, in the dying is rare, but it causes havoc when it does occur. It may be missed in the early stages because the possibility is not considered unless the patient has a past history of manic–depressive illness. Most commonly it is a reaction to steroids, and since these are often given to a patient with a primary or secondary brain tumour, the differential diagnosis lies between the effects of the tumour itself, the medication, and a psychogenic psychosis related to the stress of the illness. Usually, prompt action is needed to bring the condition under control, and both reduction of steroids, especially if the patient is on a high dose, and the use of haloperidol may be justified. In one patient the hypomania developed slowly over several weeks. She slept little and seemed compelled to spend the night cooking, making an incredible mess all over the kitchen. She bought many new and expensive clothes, ordered two wedding cakes by telephone, and could not be trusted alone for a moment. Her husband, fearing that she would be admitted to a psychiatric hospital and die there, tried to conceal the problem and cope alone, becoming utterly exhausted and at his wits end. In this case the problem seemed to be a steroid effect. Once the dose had been reduced to about half the previous level, the haloperidol which was used initially was withdrawn without a recurrence of the abnormal mental state.

Mrs G. had a malignant brain tumour. When she came for a routine consultation with her radiotherapist, he decided to admit her to his ward because her manner seemed very strange and euphoric. She had come to know her prognosis only a few days before, and her husband thought the change in her was in some way related to this. On the ward she became inexplicably aggressive and threw a pot plant at the sister, whereupon I was called to help.

She told me that she knew she had a brain tumour and that it could not be removed, but she said that it did not affect her and she knew she would live to be 88. She said this in a gleeful, almost triumphant way, unlike the usual quality of speech when the patient is using denial. As I took a further history, she told me of a series of disasters that had recently overtaken her family. Her mother had cancer and would soon die; one of her sisters had a baby with cancer and he was not expected to live for long either. Worst of all, her brother in the RAF had just been killed in a helicopter crash. She had seen it on the television – although the family denied that it was true, they were only saying that to spare her from worry. When I expressed some scepticism that so much should happen to a family in so short a time, she became angry and I hastily decided not to pursue that line any further. She was affable as she gave me other parts of her history, and agreed to take some tablets I prescribed, more to humour me than because she thought she needed them.

The next day she was calmer and tension in the ward had diminished, but her delusions were unchanged. She had asked her husband to make sure she did not have to see the psychiatrist again, and I met him to discuss her request that evening. He was indignant that I had been consulted. 'My wife's problem is a tumour, not madness', he said. I asked him for more of her history and he told of a struggle against many odds in adolescence and through a first disastrous marriage. He said she was a woman of great courage and determination who could not bear to let anything defeat her. I speculated that her 'madness' had developed because she could not bear to acknowledge that the problem of her tumour could not be solved, however determined she was to fight in her usual way. He thought there might be some sense in that. I tried to explain to him that if a person cannot cope with the idea that something is happening to themselves, they sometimes imagine it is happening to someone else instead. He found that harder to take, but admitted his perplexity about why his wife had suddenly invented these stories. He did not know how to respond to them, and the rest of the family had decided not to visit her because they were so upset by her talk. I told him gently that if I was able to make her better, she would lose these ideas but become very sad instead, because she would accept that she was going to die. At first he forbade me to try to do this, but on reflection he recognised that he would feel closer to her if she were sane, and he would be able to comfort her.

This is exactly what happened. The haloperidol I gave initially made her more accessible to conversation and she told me her life story herself. Together we shared how painful any kind of defeat was for her, and how tragic it was that she might soon die when she had only recently found happiness in this second marriage. She wept, and when some of the ward staff saw the intensity of her sorrow they wondered if they had done right to call me in. But she could be comforted and her husband sat with her as they shared the grief that he had kept to himself for months, and she had avoided. She remained aware of what she had said when she was deluded, and solved the problem of how to acknowledge the truth without losing face in an intriguing way. She explained that her family told her 'all those lies' because they thought she would feel very lonely if she was the only one with cancer. It was wrong of them, she said, but they did it out of kindness.

During the manic episode she had been using the mechanisms of denial and displacement. That these occurred in a setting of euphoria rather than the more usual one of paranoia was conditioned by her previous personality. Both she and her husband told me that she coped with everything by being determinedly cheerful, and that never before had she let anything make her cry as this had done. It is not surprising that she had to break down before she could experience the more appropriate response of sorrow. Her grief was overwhelming for only a few hours, although it returned forcefully from time to time, particularly as she became able to speak openly with her family about what lay ahead. Within a week her mental state was sufficiently near to normal for everyone to feel that she was well enough to be discharged. Her husband decided to give up his job and devote all his time to nursing her, for the tumour was obviously progressing rapidly and he wanted to give her as much love as possible during her last few weeks. I never knew the end of the story, for he took her to their favourite holiday cottage in Scotland, where he hoped he would be able to care for her himself until her death.

Hysteria

The full picture of conversion hysteria is not common in dying patients. When it does occur, it may be the result of a combination of circumstances for the patient that makes the knowledge that he has a terminal illness intolerable. To him at that moment even a very disabling symptom is preferable. One patient like this became mute within hours of being told that she had cancer, as if something unspeakable had now happened. Other patients develop bizarre symptoms at critical times in their illness, and these are often difficult to diagnose as it is natural to assume that they constitute some rare complication of the original illness. The patient's lack of anxiety gives a clue, as does the occurrence of the new symptom at a time when it will serve a purpose, for example just when the patient is thought to be ready for discharge or a visit home. The most perplexing for us has been hysterical coma: it seemed in retrospect as if the patient was indulging in a dress rehearsal of dying; perhaps to explore what it would be like, how her family would respond, and how we would nurse her. Time, and care that was kindly but that also made it clear that we did not think that death was imminent, sufficed to bring about resolution.

Dying patients who have a hysterical personality behave as they would at any other time of illness or stress, and their management should not be altered just because they are now facing death. To give in to the manipulative efforts of this kind of patient does not seem to make him any happier, but it does make him unpopular and causes undue stress to those around him. The care-giver who can be consistently kind and accepting of the fear and need that lie behind his behaviour may sometimes be able to help him to change even at this stage in his life. One woman who had tried our patience over many weeks, sensed that no one liked her very much and said so to one of the nurses. That nurse had curbed her tongue on several occasions and given the patient much considerate care and attention. This time she said quietly, 'If you behaved a bit better, we would all like you a lot more.' Those words went home, probably because they were said with love as well as anger, and the patient recognised their truth. The last few weeks of her life were easier for her and everyone else as a result.

A conclusion

The survey of the psychological detours that patients may make, as charted in the diagram in Chapter 9 (Fig. 9.2), is now complete. The fact that the patients who have these conditions may not have long to live should not deter anyone from offering treatment, for we have seen that a gratifying response can sometimes be obtained. These conditions can be seen as ways of coping with the crisis of mortality: maladaptive ways, causing unnecessary suffering, but the best the patient can do in his own peculiar circumstances. Those who care for him serve him best when they strive to understand what is happening, and, through drugs or psychotherapy or both, help him to find his way back on the route again toward acceptance. We are born mortal, and are as well equipped to cope with dying as we are to cope with all the other major changes encountered through life. When coping fails, it means that something is interfering with the natural process. The therapist tries to help his patient to clear away the obstacles so that he can proceed again unhindered, toward a goal of living well while he is dying, and dying well when his moment comes.

16

Bereavement: typical grief

Introduction

So far in this book, the dying person has been the centre of concern. Now attention turns to those who are left when he has gone. Unless death came unexpectedly, their lives will have been increasingly taken up with him in the preceding days or weeks. Suddenly there is a large space where he was. Instead of visiting and caring, there are funeral preparations marking the end of one life and the beginning of a new phase for the others. They must turn toward the tasks of bereavement: to recognise fully that he is dead and will not return, to grieve over their loss and loosen their ties to him and let him go, so that they can reorganise their lives and live well again without him.

We have already traced the journey the dying person makes, noting that there are many detours *en route* and that some people fail to reach the psychological and spiritual destination of acceptance before death occurs. For the bereaved, the end-point of their journey is less sharp, but they are equally likely to suffer if progress is impeded or they are diverted for too long from their most appropriate course. This chapter will be concerned with typical grief, and the next with the complications that arise when mourning does not proceed as it should.

Grieving is a natural process through which many people progress using their own resources, usually with the help and support of family and friends. Those professionals who have been most intimately involved with the care of the dying person want to continue their contact with his family for at least a short time if they can. They have their own grief over his death, and seeing that those closest to the deceased are set on the road to successful mourning is their final service to him. Then, if they are not normally concerned with the care of people in the community from which the patient came, their involvement ceases. At least one of those who *are* concerned – the general practitioner, district nurse, social worker, or parish priest – should continue to act as a monitor, remaining as a supportive figure in the background if all is going well, but ready to intervene if the bereaved person's needs are not being met.

A major bereavement is a bewildering and sometimes very frightening experience. Anyone who has never been through it before is prone to fear being overwhelmed and needs someone who can help him to bear it. That person must be able, by listening and talking, to help the bereaved to understand what is happening to him and to accept that it is normal and necessary, provided, of course, that it is. If it is not, the helper must be able to intervene competently himself or be prepared to refer the grieving person on for more specialised treatment. To fulfil these functions it is essential that the helper be familiar with the processes of grieving. In addition, knowing some of the origins and causes of symptoms can make the task easier for both parties. People need to make sense of grief. For many, anxiety and self-blame both diminish when they can say to themselves, 'So that is why I am feeling like this.' For this reason the description of grief will be set in a context which makes it more understandable and provides a rationale for treatment when necessary.

Helpers for the bereaved come from most of the caring professions and also from among non-professional people whose life experience, often supplemented by some training, has begun to equip them for this kind of work. This chapter is written as if the helper is a doctor, but much of it could apply with only minor modifications to any of the others mentioned.

All grief, from the most trivial to the most severe, is disabling. Even breaking a cup while washing up causes a momentary emotional response and an interruption in the flow of the activity that was going on. Much more may happen if the cup was precious, perhaps a gift from a special friend, or if it was broken deliberately or through negligence. These two components of grief, emotional response and interruption of customary and expected activity, both vary in their magnitude and duration. There is no easy way of deciding what is normal and what is not, and at what point some kind of intervention or treatment is required. The description and classification of grief to be used here, drawn mainly from the work of Parkes,[1] impose a framework on the subject to make it manageable. The manifestations of grief lie on a scale or spectrum, from a momentary response to the broken cup right through to breakdown in function requiring admission to hospital. The divisions, though of practical use, are inevitably arbitrary and overlapping, and this should be remembered throughout.

Typical grief

Numbness and disbelief

Immediately after the death of a very close relative or friend, and before the onset of acute grief, the newly bereaved person may experience an interval of numbness. Intellectually he accepts what has happened, but he feels nothing. He and those around him may be aware of the incongruity of his response. Usually it lasts only hours or days, but it is not generally regarded as abnormal unless it persists beyond two weeks. During this period such a person carries out the necessary practical tasks appropriately but feels cut off and unreal, as if he is doing it all in a dream. Occasionally one member of the family, upon whom the main burden of organisation falls, may almost deliberately control or delay his grieving, at least until after the funeral. He may be naturally solitary, preferring to grieve alone. Provided he allows himself the opportunity to do this, the delay does not necessarily have an adverse effect. But the role of 'practical coper' may be taken up as a defence against the suffering of grief. It will be rationalised on the grounds that 'someone had to stay calm when everyone else was upset', but such a person may delay grieving for too long, with serious consequences. He needs help to recognise that although it is understandable to wish to avoid grief because it is so painful, it is nevertheless a natural and necessary response to the ending of a close relationship. Anyone who can help him to start grieving, perhaps by prompting him to recall some of his most precious memories of the deceased, will do him a service.

Disbelief is different from numbness. The latter is a common reaction in the first few hours or days, when the newly bereaved may say 'I just can't believe it', and my recognise for themselves that the painful truth has not yet 'sunk in'. It has a protective function, allowing the person to assimilate over a period of time the full impact of what has happened to him, with its implications of grief and loss and consequent major changes in life-style. It may take months to accept the finality of death. Particularly where there have been long separations before, the bereaved person comes to realise that he has been assuming that the deceased has only gone away. He then suffers renewed grief when at last he realises that there will be no return.

As soon as the person begins to both feel and know that the death has occurred, the stage is set for the process of grieving to begin.

Acute grief

When a close relative or friend dies, the bereaved person has lost an attachment figure: someone to whom he has become bonded. Early bonding, typified by the attachment of a small child to its mother, is essential for physical survival. The mother provides food and safety, and also the emotional interaction so necessary for growth. As a person matures, he becomes more able to care for himself in a physical sense, and he takes his place as a member of a family or group within a society where the tasks of providing everyone with sustenance and safety are shared among a number of people, and none is wholly independent. Attachment continues, extending from mother to include father and then siblings. Later a spouse, children, and friends partially or wholly replace the early figures, and the person becomes attached to them with an intensity which diminishes only slowly as he progresses through life. The death of any of these people evokes a fundamental group of responses to separation, which are very powerful and almost irresistible because they are a part of our biological equipment for survival.

The newly bereaved person often experiences an *urge to cry out* loudly. This is derived from the need to signal to the mother that the offspring is lost or hurt, and it enables her to find him more readily. It allows the distress to be known, so that others come to help, and it also brings the relief that accompanies the expression of powerful emotion. In societies and families where noisy lamentation is unacceptable, the bereaved person attempts to restrain this urge to cry, and wears the tense and haggard expression of silent grief.

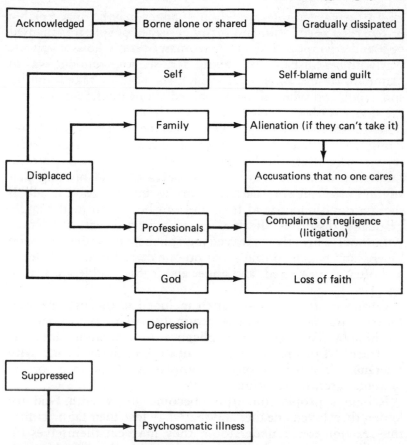

Fig. 16.1 Anger in grief.

Loss of an attachment figure leads to *searching*, and the bereaved are often prey to a powerful and irrational urge to try to find the person who has died. They may be perplexed by this, because they know he is not there, yet they go repeatedly to the grave, or to his room or other places where they feel he might be found, and they are repeatedly disappointed. This leads to *anger* that he has gone, an aspect of grief that we tend to neglect at the present time (Fig. 16.1). The dictionary definition of the verb 'bereave' is 'to rob; to dispossess, particularly of immaterial things' and 'to leave desolate'. The bereaved person suffers a sense of outrage. He has been robbed of someone precious and much of what he hoped for in the future has suddenly gone. Like loud lamentation, the expression of anger may be unacceptable or regarded as childish, and many bereaved people are ashamed of it and attempt to hide it. A woman told me how angry she was with her husband for leaving her. She knew no one was to blame for his death, and yet she felt the need to 'take it out on someone', and when alone she paced about her house, kicking the doors. Other people with less insight displace their anger onto those around them. They become irritable with their family and with anyone who wants to help them. This is why trying to comfort the bereaved can be such a thankless task; they only want the return of the deceased, and nothing that anyone offers in consolation seems to be any good at all. If those around understand this, and can bear with it, the anger gradually dissipates. If they are too hurt by it, they may withdraw. Then the bereaved person becomes alienated and lonely, and begins to think that no one cares for him. He feels, and often is, neglected, and anger about this is added to that of his grief.

Caring professionals are often included in the anger; sometimes with a measure of justification if there has been a delay in reaching a diagnosis, or negligence in providing adequate treatment. If this response is not dealt with honestly and with tolerance, it can lead on to complaints about care, or, in extreme cases, to litigation.

Religious people sometimes become angry with God for letting their loved one die, and they may lose their faith. Unless this reaction too is understood, they may cut themselves off from clergy and friends who could do a great deal to help them. In others, a temporary loss of their accustomed sense of the presence of God, and an inability to pray, often occurs and adds to their distress.

The wish to make sense of the death and/or to find someone to blame, often results in the bereaved person going over and over in his mind the events that led up to it. This behaviour also has the function of making the death real: allowing it to 'sink in'. In the process he remembers instances where he might have done or said something differently, or where he in some way hurt or upset the deceased, and he wonders if, and how much, he is to blame for the death. When anger and blame are turned onto the self, they lead to the sense of *guilt* that is so commonly a part of grief.

When none of these things happens, and the anger is suppressed, psychosomatic illness may occur later on, or the patient may present with an apparently unrelated psychiatric illness – most commonly depression.

Anxiety is a prominent feature of acute grief. It is part of the alarm reaction to loss of an attachment figure, and also a result of the insecurity that follows when customary patterns of activity are disrupted. Our sense of security derives partly from being able to take for granted many of the sequences of everyday life where a given stimulus evokes a predictable response: S→R. When it does not, we are momentarily disconcerted, or worse. Thus for 12 years the ring of our doorbell was followed by enthusiastic barking. Then our dog died, and the ring was followed instead by a loud silence, reminding us that she had gone: S→R̸→! Over and over again throughout the day, a bereaved person has experiences like this, which stop him in his tracks and leave him feeling lost and ultimately exhausted. So many things he was used to doing were initiated by the other person, or done for them or with them, and suddenly that person is no longer there. The routine of life has broken down and purposeless agitation or miserable inactivity takes its place, until with time a new routine emerges (Fig. 16.2).

Fig. 16.2 Agitation in acute grief.

This *agitation* is partly a result of conflict between the urge to search for the deceased, already described, and the opposite one to avoid the pain which follows an encounter with anything that acts as a reminder of the deceased. The vicious circle that ensues accounts for the *restlessness* of grief, with its attendant inability to settle down and do anything constructive.

As the reality of the loss becomes increasingly recognised, *pining* begins. The bereaved person experiences intense longing for the deceased, becomes preoccupied with thoughts of him, and almost overwhelmed with waves of sorrow: the so-called *pangs* of grief. These last from a few minutes to an hour, and return several times during the day, especially when offers of sympathy or other encounters or events serve as reminders of the loss. They are intense and frequent for the first week or two, and then gradually begin to subside. *Bodily sensations* and responses are prominent, due to over-activity of the autonomic nervous system. Respiration takes the form of deep sighs. Appetite is lost and the bowel function is disturbed, resulting in diarrhoea while anxiety is most prominent, and constipation later when depression supervenes. Other digestive upsets are common, and if the deceased had a gastrointestinal complaint, the bereaved may begin to think he is suffering from the same condition, especially as some weight loss is common. Similarly, the palpitations that often accompany anxiety may be misinterpreted as evidence of heart disease, especially if that was the cause of the patient's death. From these illustrations it is easy to see how *transient hypochondriasis* may be part of the normal response to bereavement. Insomnia is usual, with restlessness both day and night, followed in the more depressive phase by feelings of *overwhelming fatigue*. Particularly if the patient was nursed at home and the relatives have been on call for many days and nights, their vigilance does not cease with the death. They sleep fitfully and in their dreams think they hear the patient calling them.

An *awareness of the presence of the deceased* is common in the early stages of grief and can be seen as an attempt by the psyche to mitigate the sense of loss. This sense of presence may be comforting, and the bereaved person may talk to the deceased and feel as if he knows what the reply would be. Hearing his voice is also normal, though less common. Misinterpreting sounds as his footsteps, or momentarily mistaking a face in the crowd as his, is followed by disappointment as the realisation dawns that he is not actually there. True *hallucinations* occur too, and reassurance should be given that these are normal and not a sign of impending insanity.

Taking on attitudes and mannerisms of the deceased also occurs and can be seen as a way of making sure, through identification with him, that he is not wholly lost. The persistence of symptoms from which he previously suffered is not a part of normal grieving, although its transient occurrence requires only reassurance.

Gradually the symptoms of acute grief begin to give way. The rituals of the funeral, the need to dispose of the deceased's possessions and to deal with his unfinished business all help the bereaved person to accept that he has really gone. Then anxiety and the pangs of grief become less prominent and their place is taken by the depression and despair which characterise mourning.

Depression and despair

During this phase the bereaved person may feel hopeless and apathetic. He loses his sense of purpose and proceeds with the essential routines of living with no interest or pleasure. He tends to withdraw from others, especially if they remind him of the deceased. The days all seem the same and he does not see any prospect of change. Reassurance does not help him, and those who care for him must wait patiently, keeping him company but not pushing him too much, until they see the first sign that he is beginning to recover. This may take months. Then, to his surprise, he begins to feel better. He is pleased to accept an invitation out, and no longer goes just for the sake of the person who invited him. He decides to buy something new or to re-decorate a room. His grief work is coming to an end and he is now on the way to gaining a new identity and life-style.

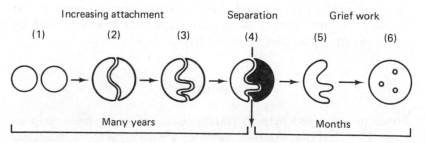

Fig. 16.3 Grief work.

Grief work is a term for the activity, both in the obvious processes of mourning, and in intra-psychic re-adjustment, which is absolutely essential for resolution. A patient of mine, whose husband had told her on no account to grieve for him, wanted to obey his injunction and carry on as if nothing had happened. Needless to say, she was not getting on very well. In trying to explain to her why it was so necessary for her to grieve, I thought of the diagram in Fig. 16.3. When you both met, I told her, you were two separate individuals (1). Over the years, through many ups and downs, you gradually adjusted to each other, so that you fitted neatly together (2 and 3). Then he died (4), and you were left in a very painful shape (5), with 'raw' surfaces which had once been close to him. The healing of grief work will come as you move from (5) to (6), and become a rounded person again. Notice that you will grow bigger than when you began (1). You will take into yourself some of his characteristics. For instance, whereas he was the disciplinarian and you the comforter for the children, now you have to do both. You did the sewing and he fixed the car; now you have to attend to both. These are big changes you are having to make. Stages (1) to (3) took many years, but the transition from (5) to (6) has to happen over a period of months, so you should not be surprised that you find it very stressful, and sometimes want to avoid it.

These drawings immediately made sense to her, and I have often used them since for others. They serve to illustrate also why things go wrong if at stage (5) the bereaved person looks for a substitute to assuage his grief. For instance, when a woman who has miscarried quickly starts a new pregnancy; parents who have lost a child promptly foster another; a bereaved adolescent marries a parent substitute; or a widow or widower remarries too soon; inevitably an attempt is made to fit the new person into the space left by the deceased. This is harmful for all concerned. It is infinitely preferrable to wait until stage (6) is reached, with its readiness for a completely new relationship.

Resolution

Some people need help to start grieving. Others need help to stop. They feel that in some way they are disloyal to the deceased if they begin to enjoy life again, and they may respond to a reminder that he or she would not want them to continue in perpetual grief. Other people remain cocooned in the withdrawal of grief because, lonely and miserable though it is, it spares them the stress of adjustment to a new role. It takes courage to go out and make a new social life alone, to accept the very different status of widowhood or single parent. Only gradually do the feelings of anxiety and insecurity give way to a new confidence. This process of beginning again can be made easier with the support and friendship of others who have had a similar experience, either informally or through an organisation such as Cruse. Many bereaved people will always remain lonely, for it may not be possible for them to find another relationship as fulfilling as that which has been lost. Others develop in new ways, almost as if the old relationship, though satisfying many mutual needs, nevertheless inhibited the bereaved individual from reaching his full potential. When his grieving is over, he behaves as someone released, and surprises himself and his friends as he discovers new interests, or takes up again pursuits that had been long pushed aside by the demands of earning a living and raising a family. For some the discovery that one can survive and even grow through a major bereavement adds strength to the character and allows them to live with more equanimity than before. This is the ideal outcome, but there are many complications and hinderances to the completion of the process of grieving. The recognition of these is important, as timely intervention may relieve some of the increased suffering, and allow the process to move on again, nearer to resolution.

Reference

1. Parkes C. M. (1972). *Bereavement*. Harmondsworth: Penguin.

17

Bereavement: complicated grief

The complications of grief fall into two groups: those which are variants of the typical process already described, where grieving is delayed, inhibited, or prolonged; and those problems that may accompany the grief reaction and partly obscure or replace it.

Delayed grief

Delayed grief is said to occur when more than two weeks elapse before grieving begins. The process may be started off, even many years later, by another loss. A patient referred because she 'went all to pieces' when her dog died, was surprised by the severity of her reaction. The history emerged that she had not mourned the death of either of her parents, two and three years before. When she was helped to recognise the connection between her current feelings and their deaths, she became preoccupied with the latter, and typical grieving for them began. Grief which has been delayed is more likely to be severe and take a chronic form when it does find expression.

Inhibited grief

In inhibited grief the person seems to be very little affected by a major bereavement, and the picture of typical grief never emerges. This occurs in some young children and there is evidence to suggest that in these cases there is an increased likelihood of psychiatric illness later in life. The elderly are also less disturbed by bereavement than are the under 65s. They seem to be less intensely involved in relationships and more self-contained, which is perhaps part of the natural preparation for loss and death in old age.

Some people whose grief is inhibited or delayed cope fairly well. They may develop a life-style designed to avoid reminders of the deceased. Other evidence that all is not well may be irritability and hyperactivity that is not satisfying or constructive. Others present with psychiatric symptoms, depression being the commonest, and the link with the recent bereavement may not be recognised either by the patient or the doctor. Psychotropic drugs are not usually effective in these cases and treatment using the technique of guided mourning is indicated. Here the necessity for grief work is explained to the patient and he is asked to allow himself to think about the deceased, however distressing this may be. He is encouraged to bring to the therapy sessions photographs and other reminders, and to go over the events leading up to the death. Some of these patients show an idealisation of the dead person which is a defence against the anger they feel toward him for abandoning them. This needs to be brought into the open and expressed. The support of a strong transference relationship with the therapist helps them to go through the process, and research shows that they do better if they involve other members of their family also.

Chronic grief

There is no real answer to the question of how long it takes to get over a major bereavement, for it is a gradual process. Although in typical grief the pangs noted in the acute stage become less frequent over a period of weeks, they tend to return with surprising force when some special reminder of the deceased is encountered. The first Christmas alone, birthdays and the anniversary of the death, are often marked by a temporary resurgence of sorrow. Consultation rates at the GP's surgery rise around the time of the anniversary, and the patient is most appreciative if the doctor can recall and share the memory that it all happened at this time last year.

Chronic grief not only goes on longer than expected, but is usually also more severe. The patient presents many of the features of recent bereavement although years have elapsed since the event. An important determinant of this is the nature of the relationship with the deceased. Figure 17.1 extends the drawing in the preceding chapter (Fig. 16.3). The partners (A), though deeply involved with each other, have many other interests which were not shared, so a good deal of their 'surface' is not left exposed by the loss. On the other hand, the survivor of a partnership where they had been 'all wrapped up in each other' (B) suffers far more disruption in his or her life when the death occurs. Those women whose interest is invested almost entirely in their spouse and/or children are particularly prone to severe grief. The relationship between a mother and a young child is also like (B). A couple like (A) may become like (B) during the last illness, especially if the patient is cared for at home and the spouse does much of the nursing. Outside interests will be dropped and nearly all the waking time devoted to the patient. After the death such a spouse feels quite at a loss at first, but often derives considerable comfort from the knowledge that everything possible that could be done has been done. After a period of intense grief and exhaustion, they may make a good recovery.

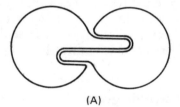

Deeply involved but with many other interests and/or attachments

(A)

All wrapped up in each other

(B)

Fig. 17.1   Varieties of relationships.

The death of a parent in old age does not usually cause undue disturbance, unless the adult child is single and has devoted his or her life to the mother or father. The death of a fully grown child seems to be one of the most traumatic, as does sudden and unexpected death, and in both of these grief is prolonged, perhaps because of the feeling of outrage which accompanies such tragedies. Where a relationship has been ambivalent, with insecure but intense attachment, there are residues of anger and guilt which hinder resolution. In all these instances, patiently helping the bereaved to go over and over the events and review the relationship, gradually breaking through defences to expose the more negative aspect, eventually allows them to come to terms with what has happened and let the past go.

Occasionally prolonged grief is itself a defence against recognising another problem which would be even more difficult to face. A widow like this was convinced that she would never get over the death of her husband, and no progress was made through guided mourning. What she could not acknowledge was her intense and possessive attachment to her unmarried son, who felt he could not leave her while she was in such a state. Attempts to confront her with this resulted in her withdrawal from therapy.

Psychosomatic reactions

Grief is never confined to the psyche. The bodily manifestations of typical grief have already been described. There is also an increased morbidity from conditions related to stress. Attacks of ulcerative colitis, for instance, may coincide with or closely follow bereavement. Mortality also rises in the recently bereaved. During the first six months after the death of a wife, widowers over 54 years of age show a 40% rise in death rate over their married counterparts, and most of this excess is due to cardiovascular disease. Patients attend a surgery more often in the first year, and this rise in consultation rate is more than could be accounted for by complaints of 'nerves' or requests for sedatives.

Psychoneurotic problems

As would be expected, hypochondriasis features here. In a transient form it is part of typical grief, but its persistence indicates the need for more help. When a patient is left alone to bring up a young family, increased concern for his or her own health is an understandable consequence of anxiety about who would now cope if he or she should fall ill. Taking on the symptoms of the deceased is an identification phenomenon seen especially in chronic grief, or as a partial substitute for grief. Just pointing out what is happening sometimes helps the patient to lose the symptom, and over-investigation should be avoided. *Phobias* too are a reflection of insecurity and are easy to understand when they are related to disease, germs, and death. *Alcoholism* may appear for the first time as a result of an attempt to gain some relief from grief, or it may be exacerbated in the already heavy drinker.

Affective disorders

It is not surprising that in some cases the *depression* of typical grief progresses to more severe forms. Here, there is a risk of suicide. Sometimes the suicidal ideas are an expression of the longing to join the deceased, and this may be tolerated and worked through with support. To other patients life really does not seem worth living, or delusional ideas of guilt or of being evil appear. These should be taken seriously and admission to hospital considered, especially if the patient lives alone.

Mania appearing for the first time within a few days of a major bereavement is far less common, but does occur. Occasionally a euphoric response is seen which is understandable. A spinster, whose life had been severely restricted for years by her elderly invalid mother, went on an exuberant spending spree after her mother's death. She came near to hypomania, but then dropped into depression and more typical grief. Other patients 'go over the top' and they require hospital admission, often on an order, as they have no idea that anything is wrong with them.

Management

The management of bereavement has been mentioned at intervals and it can be summarised thus: the newly bereaved patient needs the support of a good listener who will bear with him while he goes over events, grieves, is angry, and tries to make some sense of what has happened to him. He needs reassurance when what he is experiencing is normal, and treatment when it is not. Family and friends often give adequate assistance up to the time of the funeral, and perhaps for a few weeks more, but in many instances their attention then wanes and they assume that the bereaved has got over it. Often he has not, and it is then that the continuing support of an outsider is most appreciated. The socially isolated and those whose grief is complicated need more intense help, and for longer.

Children who have lost a parent need particular care. Often the surviving parent is so grieved he or she temporarily lacks the resources to comfort the child adequately. In addition a drop in income may necessitate moving house and/or a change in schools, separating the child from friends or a familiar teacher. It is the combination of many losses that can make bereavement exceptionally traumatic for children, and the remaining parent should be given all possible support to keep these to a minimum.

In typical grief, sedatives and anti-depressants do not usually have a place, although it may be appropriate to give a night sedative to someone who is exhausted from prolonged nursing and vigilance, so that they may recover a little before the day of the funeral. Where there is someone able to keep the bereaved person company and take over most of the organisation, talking and weeping through much of the first few nights may ultimately be beneficial, wearying through it is. Later on, if depression is persistent and disabling, anti-depressants occasionally help. They do not, however, eliminate the need for working through, a process which can be facilitated by someone experienced in counselling such patients.

Essentially, bereavement is an experience of change and adjustment, entailing considerable suffering but having within it the potential for continued maturation of the individuals concerned. The main task of the counsellor, therapist, or friend is to do his best to ensure that the outcome is as good and constructive as possible.

Postscript

The reader may be rather surprised to find 15 chapters on death and only two on bereavement. This is not because there is less to be written about bereavement, but rather that so much has been written already and some of it is very good. The medical profession has been concerned about grief for longer than it has about the care of the dying. We have now reached the stage where the many strands of knowledge that we possess about grief and loss are ready to be woven into a pattern that can be appreciated by the majority of people. This has been done exceptionally well by William Worden in his book entitled *Grief Counselling and Grief Therapy*.[1] To cover the subject in the same thorough way would be to duplicate his work, and that is why Chapters 16 and 17 offer only a brief survey with amplification of those areas where my own experience and thinking may have an extra contribution to make.

Reference

1. Worden W. J. (1983) *Grief Counselling and Grief Therapy*. London: Tavistock.

18

Professionals face death too

Most people are only intimately concerned with death a few times in their lives. Then it is a major event, and time and space are, or should be, left for them to accommodate to it. What happens to the professionals? They may be faced with one death after another, if they work in a hospice or hospital; or at least several a year if they are general practitioners or district nurses. The latter may then be losing people they have known for a long time, which may be especially saddening. What effect does this abnormal exposure to death have on us, and how do we cope?

Any contact with someone who is dying inevitably awakens some personal response. Either accepting this and working through it, or attempting to suppress it, can be stressful, leading to fatigue, over-activity, irritability, and other problems. These may eventually jeopardise effectiveness at work, and also interfere with personal and family life.

Here and there in this book, reference has been made to mental mechanisms and defences. These are not the prerogative of patients, but are double-edged tools of everyday life. Rightly used and understood, they help us to adapt and to give better care, but used excessively or negatively when acceptance and working through would be more creative, they function to our disadvantage.

One of these tools is *identification*, which is being used in its simplest form whenever someone prefaces advice by the familiar phrase 'If I were you'. Putting ourselves imaginatively in another's place increases sensitivity to their needs and can help in deciding what would be best for them. It can also lead to serious mistakes if we do not take account of the fact that 'I am not you' and can never fully know what it would be like to be the other person. Identification has gone too far when the professional care-giver ceases to recognise that he is using it and begins to think and feel like the person for whom he has become so concerned. Then he becomes over-burdened with emotion that does not rightly belong to him, and becomes less effective as a helper.

> Two families who lived close by had daughters of a similar age, one of whom was killed in an accident while out in a car with her friend. The mother of the other one imagined how she would feel if it had happened to her daughter, and for a few days would not let her go out in a car. So overwhelmed did she become by her own anxiety that she could not face her bereaved neighbour and so did not help her at all.

Doctors and nurses also identify with relatives and sometimes begin to care for a patient as if he were, for instance, their own parent or child. This may enable them to be especially thoughtful and sensitive, but carries the risk of detrimental over-involvement. Just as those who have been engrossed in a role play need to de-role at the end of it, so professional people may need to pull out of this kind of identification. Artificial though it may seem, it can be helpful to recognise what is happening and to affirm to oneself that the patient is not ones own relative; that he has become the responsibility of the next person who is to care for him, and that ones own interest and concern now lie elsewhere. It is important for those who do this work to have varied and compelling interests quite separate from their professional lives. The more a person learns to shed his concern for his patients when he is not at work, the more often and more deeply he can allow himself to be involved when he is – to the enrichment of both parties. Alternative ways of coping – by denial, suppression, or becoming 'hard' – may be just as costly in the end, and much less rewarding.

It is awareness of the hazards of over-involvement that prompts some doctors to remain aloof, oblivious that this way of preserving professional detachment denies the patient an essential ingredient of care: a good doctor–patient relationship. In my research, patients complained most about the defensiveness of doctors in the area of communication. They often perceived it as a lack of concern or even callous neglect or laziness. That may have been true in some instances, but in others it is likely that the doctor's behaviour masked his unease and sense of helplessness, or his unconscious anger at being disturbed by the suffering of his patient. In talking to those with terminal illness, some doctors manage to avoid the pain of facing it as a personal issue by rationalising (patients don't really want to know . . .), intellectualising (talking about theoretical matters like survival times or percentage cure rates), telling the truth bluntly and disappearing quickly, or delegating the job to someone else. The well-meaning doctor may take time and trouble and still not meet his patient's needs. Françoise (see Chapter 1) told how her surgeon sat with her for a long time, talking about statistics, but when he left the bedside she said, 'I still didn't know what was going to happen to *me*'. He probably felt he had done a good job, but what he had actually communicated was his unwillingness to face with her the seriousness of her prognosis. Similarly the ward round retinue that passes the end of the bed with no more than a perfunctory greeting, signals to the anxious patient that there is nothing more that they can do for him.

Doctors are not the only ones who practise this kind of avoidance. Each profession has its own variation on the theme. Nurses may maintain a brusque cheerfulness in order to 'keep a happy atmosphere in the ward'. Social workers may concentrate exclusively on solving practical problems. Clergy may offer only formal prayers or cheerful news of the parish. All may find different ways of being too busy to spend much time with the dying patient. The direct cause of these and similar behaviours may be ignorance and thoughtlessness, but the unconscious motivation is defensive, serving to spare the professional person from anxiety. We care for dying patients best when we have allowed ourselves to contemplate our own mortality, and so do not have to shy away from theirs.

The inappropriate use of the mechanism of *generalisation* poses another problem for staff. When the term is used in the way a behavioural psychologist would use it, it means that something that is learned in one setting is then believed or applied more widely. This can be an advantage, as it is in psychotherapy, for example when a very shy patient first discovers he can be assertive with his therapist, and then finds he can be so with his domineering mother also. Its use is detrimental when it is applied outside appropriate limits. This happens to some doctors and nurses who gain the reputation of being bad patients because they become unduly anxious when they are ill. This is understandable, for example for hospice staff. They work in an environment where ultimately almost every patient's physical state gets worse, and where almost all of them die. This conditions them, for what they witness around them all the time impresses them far more than anything they know in theory. 'Seeing is believing' is the colloquial expression for this. The experience of hospice staff teaches them that pain is usually due to cancer, and cancer leads to death. When they are in pain or a close relative finds a lump, it is common for them to experience an unreasonable level of anxiety, and lose sight of things they know quite well: that cancer is only one of many causes for pain, that not all lumps are cancer, and by no means everyone with cancer will die. Their anxiety springs from their experience and is therefore deeply rooted and not very responsive to reassurance alone. It can be effectively reduced to a more tolerable level through achieving insight into the way generalisation has occurred from their work setting to their personal life.

The fear of death is part of the psychological equipment for living, motivating people to avoid danger and take appropriate care of themselves and those whom they love. Fear is uncomfortable, to say the least, and leads to avoidance of situations which provoke it. Compassion, and sometimes other motives, draw people to care for the dying in spite of their fear, and they learn to overcome that part of their nature that would naturally turn away. In a sense they become used to death; not hardened, but able to cope with more prolonged exposure to it. They too have their limits, and it is essential to recognise this. One of the ways they cope is by the constructive use of defence mechanisms as already described in Chapter 9 with reference to existential denial. These are the mechanisms that enable us to live our daily lives without being disabled by anxiety about such threats as nuclear war. The assumptions mentioned there, that death is remote and only happens to people outside ones intimate circle, protect against undue anxiety about oneself and ones immediate family. When illness or death does come close and this defence is breached, there is a steep rise in anxiety for a while. It is like a stormy sea breaking through a barrier built against it, so that a member of staff who is recently bereaved or has someone seriously ill at home is more vulnerable than usual, and due allowance needs to be made for this. A few find solace in continuing to work or returning quite quickly after a death, but many need a break from other people's grief in order to concentrate on their own.

The defence that death is remote is not available to those whose work brings them into regular contact with the dying, and their unconscious sets more specific limits, like the assumption that death only happens to patients and not to staff. Accordingly the serious illness or death of a colleague causes great distress, not only because of the loss of a personal friend, but also because this defence is temporarily shattered. Those involved tend to behave like an anxious or bereaved family. Identification occurs powerfully and people say to each other, 'However would I cope if it happened to me?' The staff must then allow themselves time and space to work through this event, recognising that their professional work will seem more stressful for a time until the defences are reconstituted.

Certain mental mechanisms used by patients can cause undue stress to staff if they are not recognised and acknowledged. The two most important are displacement and projection. *Displacement* is disturbing when the patient's anger about impending death, delayed diagnosis, or the general unfairness of fate, is directed at staff who are accused of negligence, inattentiveness and lack of care. Psychotherapy may help him to express this anger and direct it more appropriately, enabling improvement to take place. Sometimes this is not possible and then it is essential for staff to realise that such anger should not be taken personally. By bearing it, but also detaching themselves from it to some extent, they ease the patient's pain.

As already described in Chapter 15, patients use the mechanism of *projection* when they cannot tolerate the knowledge 'I am dying', and project it out onto others either symbolically by saying things like 'You are stealing my money', or more directly, 'Your injections are killing me'. Again psychotherapy or sometimes medication will help the patient to accept that he is dying, and the accusations cease. But this cannot always be achieved and the nurse who does not understand this mechanism can actually begin to doubt if she is doing the right thing when she administers the medicines which the patient thinks are making him worse or are likely to kill him. If he should happen to die a short time after she has given him an injection, and his accusation is ringing in her ears as she goes home, she may be very distressed, wondering if he was in fact correct. Inexperienced staff need special support here, and it may be right for their seniors to administer drugs when this situation occurs rather than subject them to this very disturbing stress.

Goals and ideals

Those who are particularly attracted to the work of caring for the dying often have very high ideals, and these also can be a source of undue stress. Satisfaction in work depends on having an appropriate gap between ideals and performance. Where the former are set too low and are easily achieved, complacency and boredom may result. When they are about right, they act as a stimulating challenge; but pitching them too high results in a sense of failure and guilt, leading to poor morale. There are two aspects to this: what we expect to achieve with and for our patients (treatment goals) and what we expect from ourselves (personal ideals).

Treatment goals

Techniques of symptom control have improved so much that there is now a tendency to regard complete relief of suffering as a realistic goal, and to view any departure from this as a failure. Because pain control is usually achieved in a hospice within a few days of admission, staff are distressed and blame themselves if their patient is still intermittently in pain after a week. They forget that some problems are technically very difficult to manage and that some patients have psychological reasons for not relinquishing their symptoms.

Even when all physical symptoms can be controlled, it should not be expected that all emotional distress will disappear. Dying patients have much to grieve over, and for many grief work is the gateway through which they have to pass if they are to achieve acceptance and peace. Given good care and support, many people grow through suffering.

Another goal is that all death shall be peaceful. Staff may work toward this for the sake of the relatives, and indeed for themselves, forgetting that some patients remain angry that they are dying right up to the last minute. They are fighters and they want to 'rage against the dying of the light'. Witnessing their suffering is distressing, but to sedate them heavily and then call their semi-comatose state peace may be wrong. Young people especially may die like this. We were sad to see David, a father in his 20s, suffering intensely but declining all offers of help. We felt we were letting him down, but his parents thought otherwise. 'We knew he would go like this,' they said, 'he was his usual self right to the end.' That should be called success; not failure.

Similarly, family feuds do not stop just because one member is dying. They are often thrown into sharp relief as those who have not met for years find themselves around the same bedside. Sometimes a lot can be done to help, and occasionally a real reconciliation takes place. Quite often it does not and staff should not feel that this is their failure. How a person dies depends on at least three factors: the way he has lived, the type of illness, and the quality of care. Staff share grief about the first and the second, but only the third is their responsibility. Boundaries become blurred under stress and there is a tendency to lose sight of the line where our responsibility ends and that of others begins. Shouldering more than our appropriate share is moving toward an omnipotent attitude, a step toward playing God.

Personal ideals

Some professional people assume that they should naturally like all their patients or clients, and they feel guilty if they do not. We like most of our friends most of the time, but we have chosen them. We do not choose the patients who will come under our care and some of them are people whose paths would not normally cross ours, because of differing backgrounds or circumstances. There is much pleasure in widening experience through these contacts, but occasionally they will result in quite a fierce dislike which may be mutual and needs to be understood if it is to be handled constructively. The problem may lie mainly with the patient. If this is the case, confidential discussion within the staff group will reveal that other people also find him difficult, perhaps attention seeking, ungrateful, or angry. Each member of staff may be assuming that it is his or her fault, and all are relieved to discover that the problem is a general one. Sometimes such a patient should be referred for specialised help. In other instances one person may have already succeeded in gaining his confidence. When this happens, a sad or traumatic life story is often revealed which helps to explain the patient's present attitudes. Knowing the background to the problem increases tolerance. As staff become more relaxed with these patients, they also begin to relax. When such a patient has been angrily and then sympathetically discussed in a staff meeting, it is usual for everyone to comment within the next few days that he has improved considerably. If that does not happen, understanding the mechanisms he is using may help.

When only one or two people dislike a patient, the problem may be mainly with them. At times of stress this dislike can generalise, and the unpopular patient becomes a scapegoat, diverting attention from other problems, perhaps within the staff member himself. Occasionally dislike of someone has unconscious origins. They act as reminders of a relative hated in childhood or a headteacher who was feared. The person who is willing to explore further may recognise this by asking 'Whom does Mrs X remind me of?' The difficulty usually disappears when this is done, although the staff member may be left with some unpleasant memories to work through.

Not everyone has the inclination or ability to introspect in this way, and some personal likes and dislikes have to be accepted. Fortunately it is very uncommon for even the most difficult patient to be disliked by everyone, and adjusting the way care is shared out, to take account of this, is sensible.

Some people also think they should maintain the same standards of care whatever happens. They ignore the fact that their personal tolerance varies, as do circumstances: it snows; there is a strike; half the staff get flu; the water is turned off for half a day for repairs. Standards of care inevitably fall at these times, but the fault does not lie entirely with the staff, who must be able to forgive themselves when they do less than their best.

Ethical ideals

On the whole, it is senior staff, and more often doctors than nurses, who decide policy, and junior staff, more often nurses than doctors, who carry it out. This can lead to occasions when the person actually administering a treatment thinks it is inappropriate or even unethical. Unless such a nurse or houseman is prepared to say so, he or she may go home from work with an uneasy conscience, wondering if an attempt should have been made to intervene, and ashamed of timidity about speaking out. Their judgement of the situation may indeed be correct, but it is equally likely that it is based on insufficient information about the patient or the illness, because there have been no opportunities to discuss and understand the policy behind the treatment.

It is usually doctors who decide policy and nurses who know the patients best. Sometimes patients will agree to a treatment, for instance chemotherapy, because they feel they ought to comply with what they assume to be the doctor's wishes. They may then confide to a most junior nurse that they are worried about their decision and really want to change their mind. The nurse who does not pass on this information may feel very burdened by it. The working atmosphere must be such that everyone can speak out without feeling ashamed if they show their ignorance. Each person who is involved in the care of patients should feel part of the team, with the right to question what is going on if they feel uneasy about it.

Coping with stress

Awareness of the early signs of stress in individuals and groups is essential if measures are to be taken to alleviate it before it develops into a serious problem. Tiredness out of proportion to the work that is actually being done, low morale and irritability with each other are early signs. Anxiety about small things as well as large ones, and over-conscientiousness begin to appear. When demands come one after another without time to think, people tend to do things themselves rather than delegate. They muddle through, feeling tired and heroic, instead of assessing the situation and deploying the available resources more effectively. Sickness rates then increase and anxiety begins to spill over to home and family life. Spouses and children may become aware, before senior members of staff, when there is undue stress at work. People become preoccupied with thinking about patients when they are off duty, and may also dream about them. (This also happens in the early stages of adapting to this kind of work, and seems to be a normal phase through which some pass as they are confronted for the first time with so much suffering and sadness.) Under stress, the capacity to see the funny side of things and reduce tension by a good laugh may be lost, as is a sense of proportion. The scapegoating that may occur as one person or event is deemed to be the cause of all the trouble allows a release of emotion at the expense of one individual, but hinders any constructive thinking about how to deal with the real difficulty. Failure to acknowledge that there is a problem at all leads to low job satisfaction, falling standards of care, and eventually to a high turnover of staff.

Many of these difficulties arise in all settings where patients are dying, but some are peculiar to hospitals and especially hospices. In small units the workload is apt to be very variable. When there are many deaths in quick succession, staff become temporarily overwhelmed by the sheer quantity of grief with which they are confronted. If this is followed too quickly by rapid admission of new patients, they sense that they are not giving of their best. Also, at times of crisis, those patients who are most able to look after themselves tend to be neglected, and later the staff need time and opportunity to make up this deficiency. Occasionally a death is particularly tragic or poignant: a patient who is young or someone with whom many identify, or a person who has been in for a very long time. All these features increase grief. When this happens it seems right to delay filling all the beds for a day or two in order to give the staff time to gather strength and regain equilibrium. This is very difficult to do if there is a heavy pressure from outside to admit, and it is wise to share decisions about especially urgent cases. Some idealists think no one should ever complain about their work. Yet if it rains every day for a week, no one thinks there is anything wrong in saying 'Isn't it awful!'. It should be equally acceptable to complain to each other when circumstances outside our control make work unusually difficult.

So far, only the disadvantages of stress have been discussed and its positive aspects ignored. Our knowledge of the way that bones respond and grow provides an apt analogy. Too great or too sudden a stress leads to a fracture – a breakdown. But steady stress on bones, occurring in the course of activity and through the powerful pull of muscles, causes trabeculae to be laid down in a way that provides maximum strength. The stress promotes and influences the growth. It is essential that the members of all the caring professions learn to recognise stress and understand its causes so that they may care for each other in such a way that growth is fostered and very few people break. Fractures do heal, and becoming a casualty does not necessarily mean that a person is unsuited to this work, although it may. It could mean that he was subjected to too much stress too soon. Such people can become more effective if they are well supported as they work their lonely way through their own personal crisis. The stress may have highlighted a problem of their own, a vulnerability that needed to be healed and could only be reached when it was exposed. Growth and new life can come out of suffering. We must be willing to learn this first of all for ourselves. Only then will we be able to convey this knowledge with the kind of gentle communication that needs few words and enables our patients to make the same discoveries for themselves.

Index

acceptance 10
  first steps 76
  in old age 75
  route to 78, 83
acute grief 148
adjustment 11
  reaction 85, 87–92
adolescents 37
agitation in grief 151
almost certain death 44
amitryptiline 118
amputation 59
analgesics, patient's reaction 63
anger 57–8, 79–80
  in grief 149–50
  redirection 95
  suppressed 100
anorexia 53
anticholinergic side-effects
  118
anti-depressants 86, 118
anxiety,
  chronic 101
  depressive 85–6
  displacement 98
  in grief 151
  post operative 47
  post therapy 49–50
  separation 68, 102
  severe 79
anxiolytics 107
arousal level 123–4
awareness 19–22
  development 75
  filter 123

bereavement 146
biological fear of death 67
boredom 55
brain tumour personality changes
  56
breathlessness 53–4, 107

cancer
  abdominal 119
  breast 1–2, 19, 27
  bone 2–5
  colon 23, 103
  contagion fear 74
  larynx 27
  lung 22
  ovary 18
  pancreas 22, 100
  spinal cord 110
  undiagnosed 22–3
certain death 41
children, informing 32–6
chlorpromazine,
  confusion management 134–5
  dosage 44
  effect on anxious patient 43–4
  sedative effect 108
chronic grief 157
clobazam 108
cognitive stimuli 124–6

colostomy 59
communication
  husband-wife 29–32
  in adjustment reaction 87
  unsatisfactory 22–3

with children 4, 8–9
with doctor 1
with husband 3, 8–9
with parents 8–9
confusion 122–7
case history 131–4
causes 128–9
drug use 134–6
control loss 71–2
conversion hysteria 79, 143–4
counter phobia 81
crisis of knowledge of death 40,
77–9
cushingoid appearance 62

death,
almost certain 44
biological fear 67
certain 41
fears of 67–74
knowledge crisis 40, 77–9
known time 41
postponing 64–6
uncertain 47–50
delayed grief 156
denial
defence 20, 77–9
detrimental use 97–100
dependency 54, 90
depression 86
case history 109–116
diagnosis 116–118
detachment, professional 164–5
diagnosis 15–17
diamorphine 135
diazepam
dosage 107–8, 135
effect on anxious patient 43–4
disbelief, bereavement reaction
147–8
displacement, patient's 167
district nurse, home care 5
doctor-patient
contract 15
relationship 164–5

dothiepin 118
drug
-caused confusion 129
confusion management 134–6
management 107–8
dying
process 70
trajectories 41

ECT *see* electroconvulsive
therapy
electroconvulsive therapy
119–120
ethical ideals 170–171
evasive answers 25
existential
denial 76
fear 69

family
doctor *see* general practitioner
sessions 37
financial arrangements,
discussion 31
free-floating
anger 57
anxiety 101
funeral arrangements, discussion
31

general practitioner 1–2, 5, 22
generalisation, professional 165
goals for survival time 46
GP *see* general practitioner
grief 80
management 161
work 154
grieving process 145–155
guilt in grief 150

hair loss 62
hallucinations 127
in grief 152
haloperidol 108, 127, 134, 137
husband-wife communication
29

hyoscine 135
hypomania 140–143
hypnosis 107

identification with patient 163–4
imipramine 118
information to patient 15–19
inhibited grief 156–7
insanity, fear of 72–3
insomnia 102

jealousy 138–140
junior staff, communication 23–5

living-dying interval 40
lorazepam 108

manic reactions 140–143
  to grief 160
marital therapy 91
mastectomy, psychiatric morbidity 59
maternal role loss 96
mianserin 118
migraine 110
misperceptions 126–7
morbid jealousy 138–40
morphine addiction fear 11
motor neuron disease 17, 55

nausea and vomiting 106
nightmares 19
nomiphensine 119
non-attention denial 80–82
numbness, bereavement phase 147
nurse, anxiety 42

old age, acceptance development 75
over-activity 101

pain,
  fear of 70–71
  psychological reactions 52–3

relief 10–11
  tension 2, 103
pangs of grief 152
panic 42
paralysis 55
paramedical staff, communication 23–5
paranoid reactions 29, 137
parents, informing 37–9
patient
  'bargaining' 45
  co-operation 7
personal ideals 169–170
personality changes 56
phenothiazine 128
pining in grief 152
postoperative anxiety 47
pre-existing problems 12
problem-orientation 7
prognosis discussion 21–2
projection, patient's 167
psychiatric morbidity 59
psychogenic psychosis 77
psychoneurotic problems in grief 159–160
psychosomatic reactions to grief 159

regression 90
rejection, fear of 73–4
relatives' attitude to information 26–9
relaxation therapy 107
resolution of grief 154–5
restlessness of grief 152
role changes 94–6

screaming 2
sedatives,
  boredom relief 55
  effects on anxious patient 43–4
separation anxiety 68–9, 102
sexual problems, postoperative 59

somatic symptoms 79
spouse,
   accompanying patient 26
   communication with patient
    29–32
steroids, psychological reactions
   62
stoma, adaptation to 60–61
stress adaptation 171–3
sudden death, fear of 73
suicidal ideas 117

tension pain 2–3, 103–106
time of death, known 41
toxic psychosis 130
transient hypochondriasis 152
treatment
   decisions 63–6
   goals 168
tricyclic antidepressants 118

unsatisfactory communication
   22–3